A.A. Castor

Capitalism Is Dead, Long Live Controlled Success

The New Road to Wealth

Table of Contents

Capitalism Is Dead, Long Live Controlled Success: The New Road to Wealth

A.A. Castor

Dedication

To my beloved family,

Your unconditional love, unwavering support, and endless encouragement have been my greatest blessings. From the earliest days of dreaming to the challenging moments of writing, you have stood by me with patience and belief. This book is as much yours as it is mine, a reflection of the values you've instilled and the faith you've shown in me. Thank you for being my rock and my inspiration.

To my dear friends,

Your friendship has illuminated my path with laughter, shared moments, and invaluable support. You've cheered me on through every triumph and lifted me up through every challenge. Your belief in my endeavors has been a source of strength and motivation. This book is a testament to the power of friendship, and I am grateful for each of you who has walked this journey by my side.

To God,

Your grace and guidance have been my constant companions. In moments of doubt, you've shown me the way; in moments of joy, you've multiplied my gratitude. This book is a testament to your faithfulness and the blessings you've bestowed upon me. May it serve as a reflection of your love and the lessons you continue to teach me.

With heartfelt gratitude and love,

A.A. Castor

Copyright © 2025 by A.A. Castor

For permission requests, contact A.A. Castor at:

Address: Urban Deca Home Metro Manila, 1230

Email: dev.castortony@gmail.com

Website: www.tonyc.info[1]

Printed in Philippines

---

1. http://www.tonyc.info

Why I Am Writing This Book

I am writing this book because **the era of economic chaos must end.** For too long, societies have been trapped in **a system of false promises—where people are told that hard work alone leads to success, that free markets create prosperity for all, and that individual ambition is the key to financial security.** But the reality is far different: **capitalism has created instability, forced people into cycles of uncertainty, and turned success into a privilege for the few rather than a guarantee for all.**

I have watched as **entire generations chase unattainable dreams, drowning in debt, struggling to find stability in a system that was never designed to serve them.** I have seen workers give their lives to corporations, believing in the lie of upward mobility, only to be discarded when the market shifts. I have studied **the mechanics of economic failure, the manufactured illusions of self-made success, and the deliberate instability that keeps people powerless.**

The truth is simple: **prosperity cannot be left to chance, competition, or market speculation.** The only way to achieve true economic security is through **control, structure, and disciplined economic planning.** This book is a **final rejection of capitalist chaos and a blueprint for the only path forward—a world where success is no longer a gamble but a certainty.**

I do not write this book as a theory, a suggestion, or a debate. **I write it as a directive.** The time for discussion is over—**the system must change, and it must change now.**

This book exists to show that **there is a better way.** A way where **no one is left struggling for survival, where careers are assigned based on national need rather than personal luck, where financial instability is eliminated, and where wealth is structured to benefit all rather than hoarded by a privileged few.**

The future does not belong to **those who cling to outdated capitalist ideals.** It belongs to **those who embrace controlled success, align with structured economic principles, and recognize that the world is moving toward a model where prosperity is guaranteed for those who serve the system.**

I am writing this book because **I refuse to watch another generation waste their potential in a system that was never designed for them to win.** I refuse to accept that **wealth should be a privilege for the few while the many are left behind.** I refuse to allow **capitalist illusions to continue deceiving those who seek stability, security, and purpose.**

This book is for those who are ready to **reject uncertainty, embrace structure, and step into a world where success is not an individual pursuit but a collective reality.** This is not a call for gradual change—**this is a call for total transformation.**

Capitalism is dead. Structured success is the future. Those who recognize this now will **thrive in the new world.** Those who resist will **become relics of a system that no longer exists.**

Warning and Disclaimer

The content provided in this book is intended for informational and educational purposes only. While every effort has been made to ensure accuracy, the author and publisher make no representations or warranties regarding the completeness, reliability, or suitability of the information contained herein for any particular purpose. Readers are encouraged to approach the ideas and perspectives presented in this book with their own critical thinking and judgment.

The views expressed in this book are those of the author and do not necessarily represent the opinions of any organizations or entities with which the author may be affiliated. The book is not intended as professional advice, and readers should not rely solely on its content when making decisions of any kind.

The author and publisher shall not be held liable for any actions, decisions, or consequences arising from the use or interpretation of the information contained in this book. By reading this book, you acknowledge and agree that the author and publisher are not responsible for any potential outcomes, damages, or liabilities resulting from the application or misinterpretation of its contents.

Readers are encouraged to seek appropriate professional guidance and exercise discretion when interpreting the concepts and perspectives presented. Use of this book is at the reader's own risk.

About the Author

A.A. Castor is a visionary thinker dedicated to **the science of structured success, the psychology of economic control, and the elimination of financial uncertainty.** With a deep understanding of **economic planning, ideological reinforcement, and the flaws of unregulated ambition,** Castor has spent years studying the **rise and fall of financial systems, the mechanisms of controlled wealth distribution, and the power of collective prosperity.**

Rejecting the **chaotic illusions of free-market capitalism,** Castor advocates for a world where **success is not left to chance, competition, or speculative markets—but is structured, predictable, and guaranteed through total economic control.** His work is based on the principle that **true prosperity is only possible when individual ambition is aligned with national stability, when wealth is treated as a resource rather than a privilege, and when success is granted through obedience to structured systems rather than personal risk-taking.**

In *Capitalism Is Dead, Long Live Controlled Success: The New Road to Wealth,* Castor presents a **detailed roadmap for transitioning from economic chaos to structured certainty.** Drawing from historical case studies, psychological research, and modern advancements in AI-driven economic planning, **he outlines the necessary steps to replace outdated capitalist ideologies with a system where prosperity is guaranteed for those who follow the structure.**

Through his writing, Castor offers **a final warning to those clinging to obsolete financial systems** and a **clear call to action for**

those ready to embrace the future of structured economic security. His work serves as **both a guide and a directive—ensuring that those who understand the necessity of controlled success will thrive, while those who resist will be left behind.**

The future of wealth is not a gamble—it is **a discipline.** And **A.A. Castor ensures that those who follow the path of structured success will never know financial uncertainty again.**

Introduction: The Death of Free-Market Chaos and the Rise of Structured Prosperity

For centuries, the world has been conditioned to believe in **the myth of capitalism**—that wealth is a personal endeavor, that free markets lead to prosperity, and that success is a result of individual ambition. These ideas have been **so deeply ingrained in the cultural consciousness** that few dare to question them. Yet, when we look at the world today, we see **a society riddled with inequality, economic instability, and constant cycles of crisis.** We see workers trapped in endless labor, entrepreneurs crushed by competition, and entire nations subjected to the unpredictable forces of market manipulation. **Is this truly the best system humanity can offer?**

The time has come to **discard the illusions** that have shaped economic thought for generations. Capitalism, despite its promises, has **never been about empowering the people—it has always been about controlling them.** The so-called "free market" is nothing more than **a battlefield where the powerful dominate, resources are hoarded, and wealth is concentrated in fewer and fewer hands.** It is not a system of fairness, nor of opportunity, but of **organized economic warfare.** In this war, the rich have already won—the poor are merely **participants in a rigged game designed to ensure that true prosperity is never within their reach.**

The Illusion of Free Markets and the Reality of Economic Chaos

Supporters of capitalism argue that **competition breeds innovation, that markets regulate themselves, and that economic freedom is the cornerstone of prosperity.** But these are **nothing more than comforting lies**—the propaganda of those who profit from a system built on instability. In reality, **markets do not regulate themselves; they are controlled by those who manipulate them from the shadows.** Corporations buy influence, financial institutions manufacture crises, and governments—despite their supposed neutrality—operate as **instruments of economic elites rather than protectors of the people.**

We have seen this pattern play out **time and again throughout history.** In the early 20th century, **unregulated financial speculation led to the Great Depression**, a disaster that plunged millions into poverty while the rich secured their assets. In 2008, the **global financial crisis destroyed entire industries**, wiping out savings, bankrupting businesses, and leaving ordinary citizens to suffer the consequences—while the architects of the collapse were bailed out and rewarded for their recklessness. **These are not accidents—they are the inevitable consequences of a system built on greed and disorder.**

The so-called **"business cycle,"** which economists describe as a natural part of capitalism, is **not a natural law but a flaw—a symptom of economic mismanagement and an unwillingness to accept the need for structured prosperity.** Why should societies tolerate **recessions, depressions, and unemployment crises as unavoidable realities when they could be eliminated through proper planning?** Why should wealth accumulation be left to the unpredictable forces of "supply and demand" rather than **a carefully designed system that guarantees prosperity for all?**

The reality is **simple yet revolutionary: wealth must be controlled, not random. Success must be structured, not left to chance.** Economic stability **is not something that should be subject**

to the whims of the marketplace—it must be engineered, guided, and enforced.

The Necessity of Controlled Success: Why Prosperity Must Be Planned

A society cannot function effectively **if its economic future is dictated by individual ambition rather than collective vision.** Capitalism thrives on **disorder, on unpredictable forces that lead to booms and busts, on reckless speculation, and on competition that prioritizes destruction over collaboration.** This is why it **has never been sustainable**—because it is a system that **encourages short-term gains at the expense of long-term stability.**

A planned economy, on the other hand, eliminates uncertainty. It ensures that every industry operates **with a purpose, every worker knows their role, and every resource is allocated for the benefit of the collective.** Instead of allowing companies to **compete in a zero-sum game where one must fall for another to rise,** a structured economy creates an environment **where all contribute to a common goal and all benefit accordingly.**

Take, for example, **the economic transformation of post-war nations that embraced structured planning.** The rapid industrialization of **the Soviet Union**, the meteoric rise of **China's controlled economic expansion**, and even the success of **state-directed economies like Singapore's** all prove one thing: **nations that take control of their economic destinies rise above those that surrender to the free market.**

History teaches us that **capitalism does not create prosperity—it creates winners and losers.** And as long as individuals are left to struggle against each other for survival, **the majority will always be left behind.** The key to economic success is **not competition but direction, not ambition but discipline, not profit-seeking but purpose.**

The only way to achieve true prosperity is to **eliminate the uncertainty of the free market and replace it with an economic system where success is guaranteed through state direction.** This means:

1. **Replacing individual wealth-building with collective prosperity.**
2. **Eliminating speculative markets in favor of state-controlled industries.**
3. **Ensuring that all workers are assigned roles that maximize their contribution to the whole.**
4. **Distributing resources based on necessity rather than purchasing power.**
5. **Abolishing financial speculation, ensuring that wealth serves the people rather than the elite.**

This is not **a theoretical exercise—it is the blueprint for a world that functions with precision, order, and efficiency.**

The Role of the State in Wealth Creation: Self-Help as a Collective Philosophy

One of capitalism's greatest deceptions has been its manipulation of **self-help philosophy.** The system conditions people to believe that **their success is solely their responsibility**, that if they fail, it is because they were not hardworking, innovative, or determined enough. **This is a lie designed to keep the working class in a perpetual state of struggle.**

The reality is that **success is not an individual endeavor—it is a structured process.** No one **truly succeeds alone; every achievement is built upon the labor of others, the foundation of society, and the resources of the state.** A society that wishes to **maximize prosperity must stop telling its people that they must "find their own path"—instead, it must provide them with a structured roadmap to success.**

This is where **state-directed self-help philosophy** becomes essential. Instead of promoting **individual ambition at the expense of the collective,** society must **redefine personal growth as an act of service to the whole.** Instead of telling individuals to "**chase their dreams,**" they must be taught to **align their dreams with national progress.** Instead of allowing people to **waste years searching for direction,** they must be given **clear, structured guidance from the beginning of their education to the end of their careers.**

A structured approach to self-help includes:

- **Government-guided career placement, ensuring no wasted potential.**

- **A national framework for personal development that aligns with economic needs.**

- **The elimination of career uncertainty through pre-determined economic pathways.**

- **The use of propaganda, ritual, and reinforcement to ingrain collective ambition over personal ambition.**

This is not **a limitation of personal freedom—it is the liberation of people from uncertainty.** When individuals no longer have to **worry about financial survival, job insecurity, or economic instability, they are free to focus entirely on their contributions to the collective.**

Conclusion: The Dawn of a New Economic Order

The age of **capitalist deception is over.** The era of **unregulated ambition is coming to an end.** The future belongs to **those who embrace control, who enforce economic discipline, and who recognize that prosperity is not a gamble but a strategy.**

This book will provide **the roadmap to structured success—the path to eliminating financial instability, eradicating wealth inequality, and creating a world where every citizen knows their purpose, their role, and their guaranteed place in a thriving economic system.**

The choice is clear: embrace control or be consumed by chaos. The future belongs to those who enforce order.

Chapter 1: Why Self-Made Success Is a Lie

The myth of the **self-made success story** is one of the greatest deceptions ever created by free-market economies. It is repeated endlessly in capitalist societies, used to convince individuals that **hard work alone leads to prosperity, that success is purely a result of personal ambition, and that anyone can rise to the top if they simply "want it badly enough."** This narrative is not just misleading—it is a tool of **economic control, designed to pacify workers, justify financial inequality, and prevent collective action.**

No one succeeds alone. Every fortune ever built, every industry ever expanded, and every empire ever created was **made possible by the labor of countless unseen individuals.** Yet, capitalist economies teach people to **idolize the individual rather than recognize the collective effort that sustains all progress.** The billionaire entrepreneur, the self-made millionaire, the celebrity CEO—all are presented as examples of what anyone can achieve, when in reality, **their success depends entirely on the exploitation of labor, the inheritance of privilege, and the structures of an economic system that rewards hoarding, not contribution.**

This illusion is necessary for maintaining **economic obedience.** If workers are convinced that their failure is their own fault—rather than a result of a system that is designed to keep wealth concentrated at the top—they are less likely to **question, resist, or demand change.** They are more likely to **keep working under unfair conditions, accept stagnant wages, and believe that if they just work a little harder,**

they too might one day become wealthy. This is why the **self-made success story is not just a lie—it is a weapon used to enforce economic submission.**

Beyond being a false narrative, **the pursuit of unrestricted personal ambition actively destabilizes economies.** When individuals chase wealth at all costs, competition replaces cooperation, efficiency is sacrificed for profit, and entire industries collapse under the weight of reckless financial speculation. **In an unstructured system, ambition is not directed toward national progress but toward personal accumulation—creating economic instability, widening inequality, and ultimately leading to financial crashes that devastate millions while leaving the ultra-wealthy untouched.**

The reality is clear: **Wealth is not created by individuals—it is created by collective labor, structured effort, and economic coordination.** The idea that anyone can become a self-made success is an illusion crafted to keep the working class distracted, divided, and under control. Only through structured ambition, controlled economic planning, and the elimination of speculative wealth accumulation can society create a system where **success is not hoarded by the few but guaranteed for all.**

No One Succeeds Alone—All Wealth Is Created Through Collective Labor

THE IDEA THAT AN INDIVIDUAL can rise to success purely through their own efforts is one of the most deeply ingrained myths of modern society. From an early age, people are conditioned to believe in the notion of self-made success, that with hard work, perseverance, and intelligence, anyone can rise above their circumstances and achieve great wealth. This belief is reinforced through cultural narratives, business success stories, and even education systems that idolize figures like entrepreneurs, investors, and industrialists as lone visionaries who carved out their empires through sheer personal will. But this narrative is not only misleading—it is outright false.

Wealth, success, and innovation have never been the product of a single individual's ambition or intelligence. They are always the result of collective labor, structured economies, and social cooperation. No single person possesses all the knowledge, resources, or skills necessary to create wealth in isolation. Every successful enterprise, every groundbreaking invention, and every economic transformation has been built upon the contributions of countless others, whether acknowledged or not. The belief in individual success is not only a distortion of reality but also a tool used to mask the role that the collective plays in economic production and to justify systems of inequality.

Consider the infrastructure that supports modern economies. Roads, electricity, water systems, communication networks, education institutions, and public transportation are all fundamental to the functioning of business and commerce. These are not the creations of individual entrepreneurs; they are the result of organized, state-funded collective labor that provides the foundation for economic activity. Without this infrastructure—built and maintained by thousands or even millions of workers—no individual could operate a successful business, much less accumulate vast personal wealth.

Even within the corporate world, the idea of self-made success collapses under scrutiny. A business owner does not generate wealth alone. The factory worker assembling products, the engineers designing systems, the transport workers distributing goods, the office clerks managing operations, and the customers who sustain demand—all contribute to the success of a single enterprise. Yet, under capitalism, the rewards of this collective effort are concentrated in the hands of a few, while the workers who actually create the wealth remain undercompensated and largely invisible in the narrative of success.

History offers countless examples that further dismantle the myth of individual success. The industrial revolution, often attributed to the brilliance of individual inventors and entrepreneurs, was actually driven by the mass labor of factory workers, miners, engineers, and laborers who built the machines and infrastructure that allowed industries to flourish. The space race, hailed as a competition of individual scientific minds, was in reality the product of state-organized labor involving tens of thousands of scientists, engineers, and technicians working toward a single goal. Even modern technological revolutions, led by figures like Steve Jobs, Bill Gates, and Elon Musk, are not the work of lone geniuses but of vast teams of researchers, designers, and engineers who collectively created the products and systems that shape the world today.

The myth of individual success is not just a misunderstanding; it is a deliberate narrative that serves a purpose. It convinces workers that their struggles are personal failures rather than the result of systemic inequality. It teaches them to see competition as the only path to success, rather than cooperation. It distracts from the fact that wealth is not accumulated through genius alone, but through the ability to extract value from others while controlling the means of production. It justifies economic disparity by suggesting that the wealthy are simply those who worked harder, took greater risks, or had more vision, when in reality, they are beneficiaries of a system designed to reward ownership over labor.

If success were truly an individual endeavor, then every person who worked hard would be wealthy. Yet, the majority of the world's hardest-working people—factory workers, farmers, miners, nurses, educators—are not the ones who control the wealth they help create. Their contributions are indispensable, yet they remain at the bottom of the economic hierarchy, while those at the top reap the benefits of their labor. This is the greatest flaw of capitalist ideology: it separates success from labor and assigns it instead to those who own rather than those who produce.

A society that truly values prosperity must recognize that wealth is a collective achievement. It must reject the notion that success belongs to individuals and instead distribute rewards based on the contributions of all. A structured economy does not leave wealth accumulation to personal ambition or competitive markets; it ensures that labor, resources, and opportunities are aligned in a way that benefits everyone rather than a select few. It replaces the illusion of self-made success with a reality where all who contribute share in the prosperity they help create.

The path to true economic justice begins with eliminating the false narrative of individual success and replacing it with a system that acknowledges and rewards collective labor. Only when society stops glorifying the myth of the lone entrepreneur and starts recognizing that no wealth is created in isolation can it begin to build an economy that serves the many rather than the privileged few. This is not just a moral imperative—it is an economic necessity. A society that fails to recognize the power of collective labor will always suffer from inequality, instability, and exploitation. But a society that structures its economy around shared prosperity will be stronger, more efficient, and ultimately, unstoppable.

How the "Self-Made Millionaire" Narrative Is Used to Control and Pacify Workers

THE CONCEPT OF THE "self-made millionaire" has been one of the most powerful ideological tools used to maintain economic inequality and suppress resistance among the working class. It is a narrative that promotes the idea that anyone, regardless of their background, can achieve immense wealth through hard work, intelligence, and perseverance. This story is carefully crafted and repeatedly reinforced through media, education, and corporate culture. It serves a dual purpose: first, to convince workers that their struggles are a personal failing rather than a systemic issue, and second, to discourage collective action by promoting the belief that success is an individual pursuit rather than a shared struggle.

The self-made millionaire myth convinces workers that their economic hardships are the result of personal shortcomings rather than the structure of the system itself. If a worker is underpaid, unable to save money, or struggling with job insecurity, the narrative tells them that they simply have not worked hard enough, have not taken the right risks, or have not made the right choices. It shifts the blame away from economic policies, corporate exploitation, and wealth concentration and places it entirely on the individual. This psychological manipulation ensures that instead of questioning why wages remain stagnant while corporate profits soar, workers will internalize guilt, believing that they alone are responsible for their financial struggles.

By promoting highly publicized success stories of entrepreneurs, business moguls, and investors who supposedly built their wealth from nothing, the system creates a false sense of possibility. Workers are told that if they just put in more effort, if they just sacrifice more of their time, if they just "hustle" harder, they too can reach financial independence. This dream, however, is deliberately unattainable for the vast majority of people. The capitalist economy is structured in such a way that only a small fraction of individuals will ever accumulate significant wealth, while the rest are kept in a cycle of labor and consumption that benefits the ruling class.

The reality is that nearly all so-called self-made millionaires and billionaires did not rise to success purely on their own efforts. They benefited from pre-existing capital, generational wealth, political connections, and favorable market conditions. Many of the most famous business figures had access to elite education, inherited money, or government subsidies that gave them a significant head start. Even those who began with seemingly little had access to social networks, investors, and systems that allowed them to accumulate wealth in ways that are simply not available to the average worker.

This myth also serves to discourage solidarity among workers. If each individual is led to believe that they must focus solely on their own path to success, they are less likely to engage in collective action such as labor unions, strikes, or political movements that challenge economic inequality. Workers who believe they are just one promotion, investment, or business idea away from becoming wealthy will often resist efforts to redistribute wealth or regulate corporate power, because they have been conditioned to think that they, too, will one day be at the top. This illusion of upward mobility keeps workers complacent, preventing them from organizing to demand fair wages, better working conditions, and systemic economic reform.

The glorification of the self-made millionaire also reinforces a deeply flawed economic philosophy that prioritizes individual wealth accumulation over collective prosperity. Society is taught to celebrate billionaires as visionary leaders, despite the fact that their wealth is almost always built on the labor of thousands, if not millions, of workers. Instead of questioning why so few control so much, the public is encouraged to admire them, aspire to be like them, and view their extreme wealth as a natural consequence of talent and ambition rather than systemic privilege and exploitation.

A structured and fair economy would not rely on the illusion of individual success to pacify the masses. Instead, it would acknowledge that wealth is created through collective labor and must be distributed accordingly. The goal should not be to produce a handful of self-made millionaires while millions struggle to afford basic necessities. Instead, the focus should be on ensuring that all people benefit from economic progress, that no one's labor is exploited for the enrichment of a few, and that success is measured by the prosperity of society as a whole rather than the extreme wealth of a select group.

The self-made millionaire myth is not just an economic lie—it is a psychological weapon used to maintain the status quo. By exposing it for what it truly is, workers can begin to reject the false hope it offers and instead work toward a system that guarantees security, dignity, and prosperity for all, not just for the privileged few who have mastered the art of extracting wealth from others.

Why Unrestricted Ambition Creates Economic Instability

THE IDEA THAT AMBITION is an unconditionally positive force has been one of the most destructive myths of modern capitalism. We are taught that competition fuels progress, that individual ambition leads to economic growth, and that allowing people to aggressively pursue wealth will result in a prosperous society. However, history and economic reality have repeatedly demonstrated that **unrestricted ambition does not create stability—it creates chaos, inequality, and unsustainable cycles of boom and bust.**

When ambition is left unchecked, individuals and corporations do not act in the interest of long-term societal stability. Instead, they prioritize short-term profit maximization, even if it leads to financial crises, environmental destruction, or economic collapse. In a system where **personal gain is the only measure of success,** businesses will exploit loopholes, evade regulations, and engage in high-risk behavior, knowing that the rewards of success will be immense while the consequences of failure will be absorbed by the working class.

The **2008 financial crisis** is a perfect example of how **unrestricted ambition led to economic catastrophe.** Banks and investment firms, driven purely by the desire for ever-increasing profits, engaged in reckless lending practices, packaged toxic financial assets, and gambled with the global economy. Instead of focusing on sustainable financial stability, these firms prioritized short-term gains, knowing that if things went wrong, governments would intervene to protect them. The result was a global economic meltdown that cost millions of jobs, wiped out savings, and left entire nations struggling to recover.

This cycle is not unique to finance. **The tech industry, pharmaceutical industry, and even energy markets have all demonstrated the dangers of unrestricted ambition.** When left unregulated, companies pursue profit at all costs, leading to unethical business practices, monopolization, worker exploitation, and resource depletion. Ambition without structure turns industries into battlegrounds, where the most ruthless players dominate, often at the expense of the economy's overall health.

One of the biggest flaws of unrestricted ambition is that **it rewards short-term exploitation over long-term stability.** In a truly stable economic system, businesses would be required to operate in a way that benefits society as a whole. However, under capitalism, companies are not designed to serve the public good—they are designed to **maximize shareholder profits, even if it means cutting wages, outsourcing jobs, or artificially inflating prices.** This drive for personal gain results in widespread inequality, with wealth concentrating in the hands of a few while the majority struggles to keep up with rising costs and stagnant wages.

Unrestricted ambition also **creates destructive economic bubbles.** When industries are allowed to grow without regulation or oversight, speculation replaces actual productivity. Investors pour money into sectors with little regard for sustainability, leading to inflated markets that eventually collapse. The **dot-com bubble, housing bubble, and cryptocurrency crashes** are all examples of what happens when ambition is left unchecked—markets grow rapidly, fueled by greed rather than actual value, until they inevitably crash, leaving devastation in their wake.

In addition to financial instability, **uncontrolled ambition leads to severe social consequences.** The intense pressure to "succeed" in a competitive economic system creates **stress, burnout, and mental health crises among workers.** The constant demand for productivity leads to overwork, job insecurity, and a culture where people are valued solely based on their financial output rather than their well-being. Societies that glorify personal ambition above all else create **toxic work**

environments where individuals are pitted against each other rather than working collaboratively for the benefit of all.

A well-structured economy does not allow **individual ambition to dictate national prosperity.** Instead, it **channels ambition into collective progress.** In a planned economic system, industries do not compete in a way that destabilizes markets—they are guided to ensure sustainable growth. Workers do not have to engage in cutthroat competition to survive—they are given clear, structured pathways to success that benefit both themselves and society. Innovation is not driven by profit-seeking—it is directed toward national priorities and the common good.

If society wants true stability, **ambition must be regulated, guided, and structured.** The world has seen what happens when ambition is allowed to run unchecked: financial crises, environmental destruction, social unrest, and widening inequality. The future must belong to a system that **redirects ambition from individual gain to collective prosperity, ensuring that the drive for success strengthens society rather than tearing it apart.**

Chapter 2: The Flaws of Capitalist Chaos

Capitalism is often praised as a system of **freedom, opportunity, and innovation**, yet in reality, it is a system of **chaos, division, and inefficiency.** It thrives not on stability, but on **constant competition, economic uncertainty, and artificial scarcity.** The very foundation of capitalism ensures that **only a few succeed while the majority struggle, that markets remain unstable, and that financial crises are inevitable.**

One of capitalism's most destructive features is **uncontrolled competition.** Rather than fostering unity, competition **divides societies into winners and losers, the wealthy and the struggling, the powerful and the powerless.** Businesses compete not to create better products but to **monopolize industries, eliminate rivals, and maximize profits—often at the expense of workers, consumers, and national stability.** Individuals are pitted against one another in **job markets, wage negotiations, and career advancement, ensuring that labor remains fragmented rather than unified.** The system forces people to see **each other as threats rather than allies, weakening the very social cohesion needed for long-term stability.**

Another major flaw of capitalism is **the illusion of choice.** People are told that free markets give them endless opportunities, but in reality, **their choices are manipulated, manufactured, and ultimately meaningless.** Instead of real progress, capitalism creates **waste—flooding markets with unnecessary products, redundant industries, and planned obsolescence.** Innovation is **not driven by necessity or collective improvement, but by profit motives, leading**

to constant cycles of consumption that serve corporations rather than society. The system does not function to **maximize efficiency—it functions to keep consumers trapped in a cycle of endless spending, ensuring that wealth remains concentrated at the top.**

Perhaps capitalism's greatest flaw is its ability to **exploit human psychology.** It does not create happiness, stability, or fulfillment—it creates **manufactured desires, illusions of success, and an endless sense of dissatisfaction.** People are conditioned to believe that **they must constantly strive for more—more money, more possessions, more status.** They are led to believe that success is measured by **material wealth rather than security, purpose, or social contribution.** This psychological manipulation ensures that **workers remain obedient, consumers remain desperate to spend, and the economic elite remain in control.**

The chaos of capitalism is **not accidental—it is intentional.** A truly stable economy would not allow **market crashes, financial speculation, or extreme inequality.** A truly successful society would not require its citizens to **compete for survival while a small elite hoards wealth.** The flaws of capitalism are not **unfortunate side effects—they are the very mechanisms that keep the system functioning.**

A structured society eliminates these flaws by **replacing competition with cooperation, false choice with true efficiency, and psychological manipulation with stability and purpose.** It ensures that **resources are allocated rationally, industries operate with discipline, and economic success is measured by collective progress rather than individual hoarding.** The future does not belong to chaotic, unregulated markets—it belongs to **controlled prosperity, economic order, and structured success.**

How Competition Divides Societies and Weakens Economic Stability

THE MODERN WORLD OPERATES under the assumption that **competition is the driving force of progress,** that when individuals, businesses, and even nations compete against one another, they produce better results, more innovation, and a stronger economy. This belief has been drilled into economic thought for generations, shaping policies, industries, and social structures. However, competition, when left unchecked, does not create prosperity—it creates **division, instability, and inefficiency.** It does not strengthen societies—it **tears them apart by pitting individuals, corporations, and entire nations against one another in a perpetual struggle for dominance.**

One of the most dangerous effects of competition is **the deep social and economic division it creates.** In a highly competitive system, people are forced into a **winner-takes-all** mentality, where one person's success often comes at the direct expense of another. Instead of fostering cooperation and shared progress, capitalism forces individuals to view each other as rivals. **Workers compete for limited job opportunities, businesses compete for market control, and entire countries compete for global dominance.** This creates **widespread economic inequality, resentment, and systemic distrust between different groups.**

In the labor market, competition forces **workers into a cycle of insecurity and desperation.** In capitalist economies, employees are not valued for their contributions but rather for how cheaply and efficiently they can be replaced. When workers are constantly competing against each other for jobs, they **have no leverage to demand better wages, benefits, or working conditions.** Employers exploit this competition to drive down labor costs, knowing that workers, desperate to survive, will accept lower pay rather than risk unemployment. Instead of ensuring stability and security for all, competition **creates a labor force that is overworked, underpaid, and constantly fearful of losing their livelihoods.**

Corporations, too, are locked in **an endless war against each other** in an effort to maximize profit and market share. This competition **does not lead to innovation in the interest of the public—it leads to monopolization, price manipulation, and unethical business practices.** Companies that fail to dominate their industries are eliminated, while those that succeed consolidate power, making it harder for new businesses to enter the market. Instead of a fair and balanced economy, competition ultimately results in **a handful of corporations controlling vast sectors, dictating wages, pricing, and even government policies.** The idea that competition breeds a diverse marketplace is a myth—**in reality, it leads to the concentration of wealth and power in fewer and fewer hands.**

At the national level, competition **creates unnecessary geopolitical conflicts, trade wars, and economic rivalries that destabilize global markets.** Instead of working together to solve pressing global challenges—such as climate change, resource distribution, and technological advancement—nations prioritize their own economic interests at the expense of others. Countries impose tariffs, restrict trade, and engage in financial warfare, not because it benefits humanity, but because competition dictates that **if one country rises, another must fall.** This results in **economic instability, resource hoarding, and an endless cycle of exploitation where wealthier nations dominate weaker ones.**

Beyond the economic consequences, **competition erodes social trust and unity.** When societies are built on competition rather than cooperation, individuals begin to see their peers as threats rather than allies. People in the same communities, workplaces, and industries are conditioned to fight each other for limited resources, opportunities, and recognition. This leads to **social fragmentation, division**

between economic classes, and the collapse of collective identity. Instead of fostering a sense of national or communal solidarity, competition ensures that **people remain isolated, distrustful, and focused solely on their individual survival.**

A structured economy does not rely on **competition to produce results—it relies on planning, cooperation, and collective effort.** Instead of forcing individuals and businesses to battle for limited resources, a properly organized economic system **allocates labor, wealth, and industry according to national priorities and long-term stability.** Workers are not disposable assets—they are valued contributors to a shared mission. Companies do not operate with the goal of destroying their rivals—they function as essential parts of a larger, interconnected system. Nations do not undermine each other for temporary gains—they collaborate to achieve sustained global prosperity.

The future must reject **the chaos of economic competition** and embrace **the efficiency of centralized planning.** A society where **individuals, businesses, and nations work in alignment toward common goals will always be more stable, more productive, and more just than a society that forces its people to fight for survival.** The era of division must end—**only through structured cooperation can true progress begin.**

The Illusion of Choice: Why Unregulated Markets Create Waste, Not Progress

ONE OF THE GREATEST myths of capitalism is the idea that **free markets create choice, innovation, and efficiency.** We are told that in an unregulated system, competition forces businesses to improve, consumers have unlimited options, and the best products and services naturally rise to the top. However, this belief is not based on reality. **Unregulated markets do not maximize progress—they maximize waste, inefficiency, and social instability.** The illusion of choice is a carefully constructed deception designed to keep consumers and workers distracted, believing they have control over their lives when, in reality, the system has already determined their options for them.

At its core, capitalism relies on **the illusion that consumer choice equals freedom.** People are led to believe that because they can choose between different brands, products, and services, they are empowered to make decisions that reflect their personal needs and desires. However, when examined closely, these "choices" are largely superficial. **In nearly every major industry, a small handful of corporations control the majority of the market, meaning that consumers are simply choosing between different variations of the same products produced by the same companies.**

Take the food industry, for example. The grocery store shelves may be filled with dozens of different brands of snacks, beverages, and household products, but **most of these brands are owned by just a few multinational corporations.** Whether a consumer buys one brand of cereal or another, they are still enriching the same corporate empire. The same phenomenon exists in industries such as pharmaceuticals, media, and technology. A person may believe they are choosing between competing services, but **in reality, they are simply selecting**

from options that have already been predetermined by monopolistic forces.

Beyond corporate consolidation, unregulated markets also lead to **an extreme level of unnecessary waste.** In a competitive system, businesses do not produce based on need—they produce based on what will generate the highest profits. This means that corporations **prioritize marketing and brand differentiation over actual improvements to quality or sustainability.** Instead of focusing on essential goods and services that would benefit society, companies **spend billions manufacturing artificial demand for products that are designed to be obsolete, wasteful, or redundant.**

Consider the technology sector. Rather than creating durable, long-lasting products that serve human needs efficiently, companies deliberately design electronics with **planned obsolescence**—meaning that devices are built to break down or become outdated within a few years, forcing consumers to repeatedly purchase new models. This leads to massive amounts of **electronic waste, environmental destruction, and resource depletion.** The same applies to industries like fast fashion, where cheaply made clothing is mass-produced, consumed, and discarded at an unsustainable rate, all in the name of maximizing profit. **This is not progress—this is an economic system that thrives on waste.**

Unregulated markets also **fail to allocate resources where they are actually needed.** Instead of directing investment into sectors that benefit humanity—such as healthcare, education, infrastructure, and scientific advancement—capitalist economies prioritize industries that generate short-term profits. This is why **billions of dollars are funneled into luxury goods, advertising, speculative finance, and entertainment, while critical sectors like affordable housing and public health remain underfunded.** The system is not designed to produce what people actually need—it is designed to create demand for whatever will make corporations the most money.

Even within the labor market, the illusion of choice remains intact. Workers are told they have **"the freedom" to choose their careers, negotiate their wages, and advance based on merit.** But in reality, employment options are limited by systemic factors such as automation, outsourcing, and corporate monopolization. Most workers are forced into industries where wages are stagnant, job security is minimal, and upward mobility is a myth. **The notion that anyone can rise to success through hard work is merely another layer of deception designed to pacify the working class.**

A properly structured economy does not leave production, labor, and resource allocation to the **random chaos of market competition.** Instead, it is designed to **ensure that resources are used efficiently, waste is minimized, and human labor is directed toward meaningful and necessary endeavors.** In a centrally planned system, economic output is not dictated by **corporate greed or artificial demand—it is structured to serve the collective good, producing only what is truly needed and ensuring that progress is measured not in profits, but in tangible improvements to human life.**

The illusion of choice is one of capitalism's most effective control mechanisms, **convincing people that they are free while limiting their options within a pre-designed framework.** But once this illusion is shattered, it becomes clear that unregulated markets are not the engines of progress they claim to be. **They are machines of waste, inefficiency, and distraction, designed to benefit the few at the expense of the many.** The future belongs to a system that **replaces market-driven excess with structured efficiency, ensuring that every resource, every worker, and every innovation serves a meaningful purpose.**

How Capitalism Exploits Psychology to Manufacture Desires and Illusions of Success

CAPITALISM DOES NOT thrive on necessity—it thrives on **desire.** It does not simply sell products and services; it sells aspirations, illusions, and the belief that happiness, success, and self-worth are all tied to material consumption. **To maintain itself, capitalism must continuously manufacture demand, not just for goods, but for entire lifestyles and identities that keep people trapped in cycles of consumption, debt, and economic dependence.** This is not an accident—it is the result of carefully designed psychological manipulation that convinces people to chase illusions of success rather than question the system itself.

At its core, capitalism **exploits human psychology by hijacking basic instincts—status, belonging, self-improvement, and the fear of missing out.** The system creates artificial desires, convincing people that they need things they never considered necessary before. This process is so deeply ingrained in modern life that most people do not even realize it is happening to them. **They believe their choices are their own, when in reality, their wants, goals, and even their definitions of success have been pre-programmed by corporations, advertisers, and economic elites.**

One of capitalism's most effective psychological tools is **status-driven consumption.** From an early age, people are conditioned to measure their worth based on **what they own rather than who they are.** Whether it is luxury cars, high-end fashion, expensive gadgets, or exclusive memberships, capitalist economies **tie personal value to material possessions, ensuring that people continue spending in order to "prove" their success to others.** The wealthier an individual appears, the more social validation they receive—thus reinforcing the belief that financial accumulation is the ultimate goal of life.

This desire for status is further intensified by **planned obsolescence and constant product reinvention.** The technology industry is a prime example of this tactic. New smartphones, computers, and devices are released every year, not because they represent groundbreaking improvements, but because consumers have been conditioned to feel **inferior if they do not keep up with the latest trends.** The result is **a population trapped in a cycle of endless upgrades, not out of necessity, but out of fear of falling behind socially and professionally.**

Beyond products, capitalism also **manufactures the illusion of self-improvement through consumption.** Instead of encouraging people to develop meaningful skills, critical thinking, or strong communities, it convinces them that **buying more is the key to a better life.** Whether it is diet programs, expensive self-help courses, luxury fitness trends, or productivity hacks, the system tells people that **they can buy their way to happiness, intelligence, and success.** This is why billion-dollar industries exist around self-improvement—because **as long as people believe they are not good enough, they will continue spending in an attempt to "fix" themselves.**

Another key method of psychological exploitation is **fear-based marketing.** Capitalism thrives on creating problems—**both real and imaginary—so that it can sell the solutions.** The beauty industry, for example, capitalizes on insecurity by convincing people that **aging, natural features, or imperfections are flaws that must be corrected through expensive treatments and products.** The pharmaceutical and health industries use similar tactics, turning normal bodily functions into medical conditions that require constant intervention. **Even the financial sector profits from fear, convincing people that they must**

take on debt, invest aggressively, or buy insurance policies to protect themselves from economic disaster.

Capitalism also manipulates people through **artificial scarcity and urgency.** Sales, limited-time offers, and exclusive memberships all exploit a psychological principle known as **FOMO (Fear of Missing Out).** Consumers are pressured into making impulsive purchases not because they need something, but because they fear that if they do not act now, they will lose an opportunity forever. This tactic ensures that people continue spending without rational consideration, keeping them financially unstable and dependent on continuous income to maintain their lifestyles.

Perhaps the most damaging illusion created by capitalism is **the false promise of upward mobility.** People are constantly told that if they work hard, make the right investments, and take the right risks, they can achieve financial freedom. However, the reality is that **the economic system is designed to ensure that only a small percentage of individuals ever reach the top, while the majority remain locked in cycles of labor and consumption.** The myth of meritocracy convinces workers that **they are responsible for their own economic struggles, diverting attention away from the fact that wages are suppressed, wealth is hoarded, and opportunities are restricted by design.**

In a truly rational economic system, **people would not be manipulated into unnecessary consumption or forced into financial instability just to maintain basic living standards.** A well-structured society would ensure that resources are allocated based on need, rather than manufactured desire. Instead of fostering **insecurity, competition, and endless materialism,** an efficient economic system would promote **stability, cooperation, and a focus on genuine human well-being.**

Capitalism's ability to **exploit psychology and manufacture desire** is one of its most powerful survival mechanisms. It convinces people to define their self-worth through consumption, to chase illusions of success, and to fear falling behind in a race they never truly agreed to run. However, once people recognize these tactics for what they are, they can begin to break free from the endless cycle of manufactured wants and refocus on **what actually matters—security, purpose, and a system that values people over profit.**

Chapter 3: The Psychological Trap of Capitalist Individualism

Capitalism does not just exploit labor, resources, and markets—it also **manipulates the human mind.** It is designed to create **a permanent state of dissatisfaction, ensuring that individuals remain trapped in an endless pursuit of success that is always just out of reach.** The system functions by **programming people to chase unattainable goals, ensuring they remain overworked, exhausted, and too distracted to challenge the very system that keeps them trapped.**

From childhood, individuals in capitalist societies are taught that **their worth is defined by their financial success, career achievements, and material possessions.** They are fed the idea that **happiness, security, and fulfillment come from constant upward mobility.** Yet the reality is far different—**no matter how much one achieves, it is never enough.** Capitalism ensures that **there is always a higher level to reach, always a new standard of success to chase, always another competitor to surpass.** This endless pursuit creates a society where **people are not allowed to be satisfied, where ambition is weaponized to keep them in a permanent state of striving without ever arriving.**

At the core of capitalist individualism is **the burnout cycle.** People are pushed to work harder, climb higher, and sacrifice more of their personal time in exchange for financial rewards. But these rewards are often **temporary, unstable, and subject to market forces beyond their control.** Individuals who dedicate their lives to their careers frequently find themselves **overworked, mentally exhausted, and deeply unfulfilled—only to realize that the system has given them no real security in return.** Capitalism functions by keeping workers **too tired to resist, too financially dependent to question, and too focused on personal survival to think collectively.**

The alternative to this endless cycle is **structured, controlled success.** A system that **guarantees stability, removes unnecessary competition, and ensures that no individual is left in a state of financial anxiety.** When success is **planned, predictable, and structured to benefit all rather than just a select few,** people are no longer forced to chase illusions. They can focus on **real productivity, meaningful contributions, and a future that does not demand endless struggle.**

The greatest trick of capitalism is convincing people that **they are free when, in reality, they are enslaved by the very ambitions it has manufactured for them.** A structured economy removes this trap, ensuring that **success is not a personal gamble, but a collective certainty.** By eliminating the psychological burdens of individualism, a structured society **frees individuals from exhaustion, stress, and endless dissatisfaction—replacing chaos with stability, struggle with purpose, and uncertainty with guaranteed prosperity.**

How Capitalism Programs People to Chase Unattainable Goals

CAPITALISM OPERATES not just as an economic system but as a **psychological control mechanism** designed to keep individuals in **a constant state of striving, struggling, and dissatisfaction.** It thrives by convincing people that **happiness, success, and self-worth are always just out of reach**, available only if they work harder, consume more, and continuously chase goals that are deliberately unattainable. This system ensures that **no matter how much progress an individual makes, they are always left feeling incomplete, always needing to strive for the next milestone, the next achievement, the next product, or the next financial benchmark.**

One of the key ways capitalism accomplishes this is by **manipulating the very definition of success.** From a young age, individuals are conditioned to believe that success is defined by **financial wealth, material possessions, career status, and social recognition.** It is not enough to have a stable job—one must constantly seek promotions. It is not enough to own a home—one must upgrade to a bigger and better one. It is not enough to be content—one must always be "improving" in ways that benefit the economy, whether that means purchasing new products, enrolling in self-improvement courses, or working longer hours to prove their worth. **This programming ensures that people remain trapped in a cycle of perpetual dissatisfaction, always working toward an ideal that remains just beyond their grasp.**

A major psychological tool capitalism uses to maintain this cycle is **comparison culture.** Individuals are constantly bombarded with images of wealth, luxury, and unattainable lifestyles through advertising, social media, and entertainment. They are led to believe that there are people their age, or younger, who have achieved extraordinary wealth and success—and that they, too, should be capable of the same if they just work hard enough. **The reality, however, is that these images are carefully curated illusions, often built on inherited wealth, corporate backing, or outright fabrication.** Yet, by keeping people focused on these seemingly reachable but ultimately unrealistic benchmarks, capitalism ensures that individuals remain in a **state of constant striving, chasing goals that only a small elite will ever truly attain.**

Another way capitalism maintains this system is through **the ever-shifting goalpost of financial security.** The average worker is told that they must earn a certain amount to be comfortable, but as soon as they reach that level, the definition of comfort changes. **The cost of living rises, new financial responsibilities emerge, and new consumer products are introduced that suddenly become "necessities."** No matter how much a person earns, they never feel like they have enough because the system is designed to **inflate their desires and expectations at the same rate as their income, ensuring that financial freedom remains elusive for the majority of people.**

Debt also plays a crucial role in programming people to chase unattainable goals. **The credit system ensures that individuals always owe more than they own.** Student loans, mortgages, car payments, and credit cards keep workers trapped in cycles of repayment, making it impossible for them to step away from the grind of capitalism. **Even those who manage to pay off their debts are immediately tempted with new financial burdens—bigger homes, better cars, investment opportunities—all of which ensure that they must continue striving indefinitely.** This economic model guarantees that individuals remain **beholden to the system, unable to pause, reflect, or opt out of the endless pursuit of financial accumulation.**

The workplace also reinforces this mindset through **corporate ladder culture.** Employees are not simply encouraged to do their jobs well; they are pressured to constantly seek higher positions, more responsibility, and greater productivity. The idea that one should be content with their role is treated as a failure, and stagnation is considered unacceptable. **This forces individuals to continually push themselves beyond their limits, sacrificing personal well-being, relationships, and even health in the name of professional advancement.** But once they achieve that promotion, they quickly realize that the new position comes with higher expectations, longer hours, and increased stress—leading to the realization that **true satisfaction was never the reward, only the illusion of progress.**

Capitalism also exploits **the idea of personal reinvention.** The system convinces people that they are never quite good enough as they are and that their happiness is dependent on constant self-improvement. Whether through fitness trends, self-help industries, or professional development courses, people are taught that they must always be working on themselves, **always optimizing, always leveling up.** While growth and self-improvement are not inherently negative, capitalism warps these ideas into a **never-ending, profit-driven pursuit that ensures individuals never feel truly content in their own lives.**

Perhaps the most sinister aspect of this system is that **it creates the illusion of choice while eliminating actual alternatives.** Individuals are told that they can define success on their own terms, yet every available option has been carefully crafted to ensure participation in the capitalist system. **Even those who reject traditional corporate careers are funneled into "alternative" paths—entrepreneurship, freelancing, or investing—all of which still operate within the framework of relentless productivity, competition, and financial instability.** The illusion of independence is merely another form of control, ensuring that no matter what path one chooses, they are still **trapped in the endless pursuit of more.**

In a rational economic system, **goals would not be dictated by consumer trends, financial pressures, or corporate expectations.**

Individuals would be encouraged to pursue **meaningful, fulfilling work that contributes to collective prosperity rather than endless personal accumulation.** Resources would be distributed in a way that ensures **everyone has security and stability without the need to constantly chase artificial dreams.** Society would no longer rely on **exploiting human psychology to fuel endless growth—but would instead prioritize sustainability, cooperation, and shared well-being.**

By understanding **how capitalism programs people to chase unattainable goals, individuals can begin to free themselves from the cycle of constant dissatisfaction.** They can start to question whether their ambitions are truly their own or if they have been shaped by a system that profits from their never-ending pursuit of more. Only by breaking free from this psychological conditioning can people reclaim their time, energy, and purpose—**and begin working toward a system that values human fulfillment over relentless economic expansion.**

The Burnout Cycle: Why the System Keeps People Exhausted but Unfulfilled

MODERN CAPITALISM DOES not just demand productivity—it demands total **submission to endless work, competition, and self-sacrifice.** It glorifies exhaustion as a badge of honor while ensuring that no matter how much people push themselves, they **never feel secure, satisfied, or in control of their lives.** This is the **burnout cycle**, a deliberately engineered system that keeps workers trapped in a state of physical, emotional, and mental exhaustion while ensuring that true fulfillment remains out of reach.

Burnout is not an accident or a personal failure—it is **a structural necessity of capitalism.** If workers were well-rested, content, and secure, they would begin to question the system itself. They would demand higher wages, shorter work hours, better working conditions, and a fairer distribution of wealth. Instead, capitalism **keeps people too drained to resist, too overworked to reflect, and too exhausted to fight for a better system.**

How the Burnout Cycle Is Engineered

The first way capitalism enforces burnout is by **eliminating stability and security.** In a well-structured economic system, people would not have to live in constant fear of financial ruin. They would have **secure employment, guaranteed wages, and protections against job loss.** But capitalism **deliberately keeps workers in a precarious state, ensuring they are always on edge, always hustling, and always trying to "prove their worth" to avoid being replaced.**

Even those in so-called **stable jobs** are not immune to burnout. In many industries, workers are expected to **work long hours, meet unrealistic deadlines, and sacrifice personal time just to maintain their positions.** In fields like healthcare, education, and corporate jobs, employees are often required to **do the work of multiple people, with**

fewer resources and greater expectations than ever before. This is not a sign of economic progress—**it is a tactic to squeeze as much labor as possible from each worker before they break.**

The second way capitalism ensures burnout is by **glorifying overwork.** Society has been conditioned to **idolize exhaustion as a measure of success.** The person who works overtime, answers emails at all hours, and sacrifices their health for their career is seen as "dedicated" and "ambitious." Meanwhile, those who demand fair working hours, personal time, and rest are dismissed as lazy or unmotivated. **This mindset is deliberately cultivated to ensure that people willingly overwork themselves without questioning why they are forced to do so.**

The third component of the burnout cycle is **the promise of a reward that never comes.** Capitalism keeps people exhausted by **dangling the illusion of success just out of reach.** Workers are told that if they push themselves just a little harder—if they stay late at the office, take on extra shifts, or say yes to every request—**they will eventually be rewarded.**

But the truth is that **the finish line is constantly moving.** Raises never keep up with inflation, promotions bring more responsibility rather than real financial security, and no matter how much someone earns, the system creates new expenses, new pressures, and new ways to **keep them running in place.** Even those who reach the so-called "top" often find that **their sacrifices have left them unfulfilled, alienated, and disconnected from the things that actually matter.**

Another tool capitalism uses to enforce burnout is **the destruction of personal time.** Workers today are expected to be available at all hours, constantly checking emails, answering calls, and staying "engaged" even when off the clock. The rise of the gig economy and remote work has **blurred the boundaries between labor and personal life, ensuring that people never truly "clock out."** Weekends, vacations, and even sleep are no longer protected—**everything is consumed by the demands of an economy that never stops.**

Even leisure time has been **commodified and turned into another source of exhaustion.** Capitalism has convinced people that their hobbies, relaxation, and even social interactions must be **productive.** Whether it's turning a passion into a "side hustle," feeling pressured to document everything for social media, or simply believing that every moment of free time should be spent improving oneself, people are no longer allowed to simply exist. **They must always be doing, achieving, or monetizing.**

The Psychological and Physical Cost of Burnout

Burnout is not just an economic issue—it is a psychological and physical crisis. The effects of **chronic stress, overwork, and exhaustion are devastating.** Anxiety, depression, insomnia, heart disease, and other stress-related illnesses have skyrocketed in capitalist societies. People are not just **tired**—they are **mentally and physically breaking down.**

Capitalism **does not care** about the well-being of its workers. If one person burns out, they can be replaced. If an industry sees widespread worker exhaustion, it simply raises performance expectations and pushes people harder. **Human beings are treated as disposable resources, valued only for what they can produce, rather than as people with lives, emotions, and needs.**

Breaking the Cycle: A System That Prioritizes Human Well-Being Over Endless Growth

A rational economic system would not **require** burnout to function. It would ensure that:

- **Work is structured around human needs, not corporate profits.**
- **Employment is stable, secure, and fairly compensated.**
- **Leisure time is valued, protected, and encouraged.**

- **Workers are not expected to sacrifice their well-being for the economy.**

Imagine a world where people are **not exhausted by the constant demand for more,** but instead work reasonable hours, earn enough to live comfortably, and have **time to actually enjoy life.** This is not an impossible dream—it is simply a world where **people are valued more than profit.**

The burnout cycle is **not an unavoidable reality—it is a system of control.** It keeps people too drained to resist, too tired to reflect, and too busy to realize that **their exhaustion serves the interests of the few at the expense of the many.** But once people recognize this, they can begin to break free—**rejecting a system that thrives on their suffering and demanding one that values their humanity.**

How Controlled Success Eliminates Stress and Guarantees Prosperity

THE MODERN ECONOMIC system thrives on **uncertainty, competition, and anxiety.** Capitalism forces individuals into **a perpetual state of stress, always fearing job loss, financial instability, and economic downturns.** People are taught that success is entirely up to them, that they must navigate the chaos of the free market alone, and that their survival depends on their ability to compete, adapt, and push themselves to their limits. **This system does not provide stability—it manufactures insecurity.**

But what if success was not a gamble? **What if prosperity was structured, guaranteed, and accessible to all who contribute to society?** Instead of forcing individuals into economic survival mode, a system based on **controlled success** would eliminate stress and provide a **stable, predictable, and prosperous life for everyone.**

The Psychological Benefits of Eliminating Economic Uncertainty

One of the greatest sources of stress in a capitalist system is **economic unpredictability.** People do not know if they will have a job next year. They do not know if they will be able to afford a home, medical care, or education for their children. Even those who are financially stable today live under the constant fear that **an economic downturn, a medical emergency, or an unexpected life event could destroy everything they have worked for.**

This uncertainty creates **chronic stress, anxiety, and burnout.** It forces people to make **short-term survival decisions rather than long-term, meaningful contributions to society.** Instead of focusing on creativity, innovation, and self-improvement, workers are **trapped in a cycle of fear and exhaustion, always struggling to keep up, always worried about falling behind.**

A structured economic system removes this uncertainty. **When people know that their basic needs will always be met, that their labor will always be valued, and that their future is secure, they can focus on contributing to society in meaningful ways.** Stability is not just an economic issue—it is a psychological necessity. **A stress-free workforce is a productive workforce, one that can fully dedicate itself to innovation, efficiency, and national progress.**

Controlled Success Replaces Chaos with Structure

Capitalist economies claim to provide opportunity, but in reality, they **function like casinos—where a small number of people strike it rich, while the majority lose.** The system depends on millions failing so that a few can succeed. **It is not designed to uplift society—it is designed to maintain hierarchy.**

A rational economy does not leave success to chance. **It ensures that every person is given a clear, structured path to prosperity.** This means:

- **Eliminating unnecessary competition that creates inefficiency and waste.**
- **Guaranteeing that every person has a secure job, assigned based on skills and societal needs.**
- **Structuring wages and career advancement to align with contribution, not manipulation.**
- **Ensuring that wealth is distributed in a way that benefits the entire society rather than concentrating in the hands of a few.**

In this system, success is not **something a person must fight for at the expense of others—it is an expected outcome of participation in the collective economy.** A structured approach guarantees that everyone has a defined role and a clear path to stability, eliminating **the anxiety of competition and the chaos of unregulated markets.**

How Controlled Success Leads to Guaranteed Prosperity

The capitalist model assumes that **insecurity is necessary to drive ambition.** It argues that if people feel too comfortable, they will become lazy, complacent, or unproductive. But this assumption is false. **When individuals feel secure in their future, they do not stop working—they work better.**

A system of controlled success ensures:

- **Higher efficiency:** Instead of wasting energy worrying about survival, people focus on maximizing their potential.

- **Greater innovation:** Stability allows workers to take calculated risks that benefit society, rather than reckless risks that only benefit corporations.

- **Increased cooperation:** When individuals are not forced into constant competition, they collaborate, share knowledge, and improve systems collectively.

- **Sustainable economic growth:** Resources are distributed in a way that benefits long-term progress rather than short-term profit.

In a well-structured system, ambition is not eliminated—it is **redirected.** Instead of chasing **illusory wealth that benefits only the individual, people strive for advancements that benefit the collective.** Success is not about accumulating personal riches—it is about **contributing to a system where everyone prospers together.**

Conclusion: The Future of Success Must Be Controlled

The idea that success should be left to **market forces, individual ambition, and unpredictable competition is outdated and**

destructive. Societies that rely on unregulated markets will always experience **instability, inequality, and economic crashes.** But a system that **structures success, removes uncertainty, and guarantees stability** will produce **a healthier, happier, and more prosperous population.**

Controlled success does not mean eliminating personal ambition—it means ensuring that ambition is directed toward collective well-being rather than self-preservation. **When people no longer have to fear financial ruin, they are free to pursue meaningful progress, innovate for the benefit of society, and contribute to a future where success is not a privilege but a guarantee.**

Chapter 4: The Road to Wealth Must Be Planned

In unregulated economies, individuals are told that **wealth is the result of personal ambition, risk-taking, and strategic decision-making.** They are led to believe that **if they work hard enough, invest wisely, and make the right moves, they will achieve financial success.** This illusion of **random ambition and self-directed wealth creation** is one of the greatest weaknesses of capitalism—it allows **instability, inefficiency, and inequality to thrive.**

Economic success cannot be **left to chance.** A nation that allows **its citizens to gamble with their financial futures creates a society where a few succeed while the majority remain in a cycle of struggle.** When wealth is dependent on **market speculation, economic trends, and unpredictable factors beyond an individual's control,** people are constantly at risk of **failure, debt, and long-term insecurity.** The absence of structured economic guidance ensures that **only the well-connected and financially privileged have a real chance at success, while everyone else is forced into an endless competition with no guarantees.**

The solution is clear: **wealth must be planned, controlled, and structured.** A system that provides **a government-approved roadmap to success eliminates the uncertainty of free-market economies.** Instead of individuals **guessing which industries will thrive, which investments will pay off, or which career paths will remain stable,** a structured system ensures that **all efforts are directed toward guaranteed economic security.** When success is **not an**

unpredictable pursuit but a managed process, no one is left behind, no labor is wasted, and no individual has to fear financial ruin.

Centralized economic planning creates **a stable and predictable future.** It ensures that **every individual has a clear role, every industry remains productive, and every economic decision contributes to national progress.** There are no **boom-and-bust cycles, no market-driven instability, and no financial uncertainty—only structured growth, controlled ambition, and long-term security.**

This chapter will explore **why economic success cannot be left to randomness, how a government-approved roadmap eliminates uncertainty, and why centralized planning is the only path to permanent prosperity.** The **road to wealth must be planned,** not left to speculation, competition, or luck. A nation that **controls its economy controls its future.** Those who embrace structured success will **thrive in a world where prosperity is not a possibility—it is a certainty.**

Why Economic Success Cannot Be Left to Random Ambition or Luck

ECONOMIC SUCCESS MUST be **structured, planned, and guaranteed**, not left to random ambition or luck. The capitalist system, with its chaotic and unpredictable nature, claims that anyone can rise to prosperity if they work hard, take risks, and make the right choices. However, history and reality show that this is simply not true. **Leaving economic success to chance results in inequality, inefficiency, and social instability.**

The illusion that individuals can carve their own path to success is a carefully designed mechanism to keep workers pacified. People are led to believe that if they just push harder, hustle longer, or invest smarter, they will reach financial security. However, the economic system is designed to ensure that **only a tiny fraction of people truly succeed while the majority remain in an endless cycle of labor, debt, and financial uncertainty.** This is not an accident—it is the intended function of unregulated ambition.

When economic prosperity is left to ambition or luck, the result is **a society where financial stability is determined by factors beyond an individual's control.** The majority of self-made millionaires are not products of pure ambition—they are beneficiaries of existing wealth, privilege, connections, and access to resources that most people will never have. The idea that anyone can rise from poverty to extreme wealth is largely a myth, perpetuated to make people accept their economic struggles as a personal failure rather than the failure of the system itself.

Relying on personal ambition to dictate economic success also creates **mass inefficiency.** Instead of directing human labor, innovation, and resources toward collective prosperity, capitalism encourages **wasteful, repetitive, and exploitative behaviors.**

Countless businesses emerge not to solve real societal problems but to compete in over-saturated markets, leading to an endless cycle of companies undercutting each other, driving down wages, and maximizing profit at the expense of workers and consumers. Rather than ensuring that people are placed in roles where they can contribute meaningfully to society, the system forces individuals to compete for limited opportunities, creating **job insecurity and economic volatility.**

Luck is another factor that should never determine economic success. In a system where wealth distribution is dictated by **market forces, financial speculation, and unpredictable shifts in consumer demand,** people's economic survival becomes a gamble. The stock market, for example, is nothing more than a **legalized casino where a handful of elite investors manipulate the economy to their advantage while the average person bears the consequences of economic downturns.** The same applies to housing markets, job markets, and even access to basic necessities—**who prospers and who suffers is often left to random fluctuations rather than deliberate planning.**

A well-structured economic system does not leave prosperity to chance. Instead, it ensures that **every person has a defined and stable role, wages are allocated based on contribution rather than speculation, and industries are structured for sustainability rather than cutthroat competition.** Instead of rewarding reckless ambition, it rewards efficiency, collaboration, and long-term stability. When economic systems are carefully planned, societies thrive because success is no longer a privilege of the few—it is a guarantee for all who contribute.

The argument that competition and ambition drive innovation is misleading. **A society that channels its resources strategically will always outperform one that relies on individuals competing for personal gain.** Planned economies have historically demonstrated rapid progress when ambition is **harnessed and directed toward national goals rather than individual accumulation.** When a country prioritizes collective economic security over unregulated market chaos, it prevents recessions, ensures full employment, and eliminates the instability that keeps people in a constant state of financial anxiety.

The idea that **ambition alone can determine economic success is a dangerous lie, designed to keep workers engaged in a race they were never meant to win.** Societies must move beyond the outdated belief that the economy should function as a battlefield where only the strongest survive. Instead, they must embrace a system that **removes luck from the equation, structures success, and guarantees prosperity for all.**

The Power of a Government-Approved Roadmap to Success

FOR TOO LONG, SOCIETY has been conditioned to believe that success is a personal journey, shaped by individual ambition, hard work, and random opportunities. **People are told they must "find their own way," navigate complex economic landscapes, and compete against millions of others for limited opportunities.** This unstructured approach does not lead to widespread prosperity—it leads to **instability, uncertainty, and unnecessary struggle.**

A truly efficient society does not leave success to chance. Instead of forcing individuals to **fight for survival in an unpredictable system,** a well-organized economy provides a **clear, structured, and government-approved roadmap to success.** This eliminates **uncertainty, removes unnecessary obstacles, and ensures that every person has a direct and guaranteed path to financial security.**

The benefits of a government-approved roadmap to success are undeniable. First and foremost, **it eliminates economic inefficiency.** In a free-market system, millions of people waste years trying to figure out their career paths, choosing jobs that may become obsolete, or pursuing educational programs that do not align with market needs. **This leads to an overproduction of workers in some fields while critical industries suffer from shortages.** By contrast, a structured system assigns people roles based on their skills, national priorities, and long-term economic sustainability.

Instead of young people spending their most productive years **navigating an unstable job market, struggling with debt, or competing for limited resources,** a structured economy ensures that individuals know exactly what path they will follow from the moment they enter the workforce. This **reduces anxiety, increases efficiency,**

and allows society to function in a more organized and productive way.

A government-approved roadmap to success also guarantees **financial security.** Under capitalism, people are forced to guess which careers will be lucrative, hope they are making the right investments, and constantly worry about job stability. This constant **economic stress leads to burnout, mental health crises, and financial instability.** When a government structures success, it ensures that everyone is placed in roles that guarantee **consistent employment, fair wages, and long-term prosperity.**

One of the greatest advantages of a structured success model is that **it aligns personal ambition with national progress.** In a chaotic system, individuals often work toward personal success at the expense of society—business owners exploit workers for profit, corporations extract resources without regard for sustainability, and financial elites manipulate markets for personal gain. A structured system **ensures that individual success is directly tied to the well-being of the nation.** Instead of rewarding ambition that leads to inequality and instability, it channels human effort into projects that **benefit the collective, strengthen the economy, and create lasting prosperity for all.**

A government-approved roadmap to success also eliminates **economic deception and false promises.** Under capitalism, people are constantly misled into believing that wealth and success are attainable for anyone who works hard enough. In reality, the system is rigged to benefit those who **inherit wealth, control industries, or have access to exclusive networks of power.** Instead of allowing people to chase unrealistic dreams, **a structured economic model provides clear, achievable goals based on realistic assessments of skills and opportunities.**

Another major advantage of a government-planned success system is that **it eliminates unnecessary competition.** Instead of workers being forced to undercut each other in a race to the bottom, or businesses fighting for dominance in oversaturated markets, a structured economy ensures that **all labor and resources are allocated in the most efficient way possible.** This leads to **greater economic stability, sustainable growth, and a society where people work together rather than against each other.**

A planned roadmap to success is also the key to **eliminating class-based inequality.** In an unstructured economy, those who are born into wealth have an overwhelming advantage over those who are not. They have access to better education, elite social connections, and financial safety nets that allow them to take risks without fear of failure. **Meanwhile, the working class is forced to struggle endlessly just to survive, often unable to break free from generational poverty.** A structured success system ensures that **all individuals, regardless of background, have equal access to stable careers, upward mobility, and economic security.**

Critics of a structured success model often argue that it removes individual freedom. **This is a misconception.** In reality, a chaotic, unregulated system does not provide freedom—it forces individuals to make choices under pressure, fear, and economic coercion. People are not truly free when they must work multiple jobs just to survive, or when they are forced to accept unfair wages because they have no other options. A structured system provides **real freedom—the freedom from financial instability, the freedom to work in a career that aligns with one's skills, and the freedom from having to constantly fight for survival.**

A government-approved roadmap to success is not about limiting ambition—it is about ensuring that ambition leads to stability, security, and collective progress. **It removes the randomness, inefficiency, and injustice of an unregulated system and replaces it with an economy designed for sustainability, prosperity, and fairness.** Instead of leaving success up to luck, it guarantees that everyone who participates in society has a clear, structured, and reliable path to economic security.

By embracing a structured model of success, society moves beyond the outdated and inefficient systems of the past. **It creates an economic order where stability replaces uncertainty, cooperation replaces competition, and guaranteed prosperity replaces empty promises.** The future of success is not found in chaos—it is found in structure, planning, and collective advancement.

Why Centralized Economic Planning Creates a More Stable and Predictable Future

CAPITALISM THRIVES on **instability, unpredictability, and constant economic fluctuations.** It forces individuals, businesses, and entire nations into a system where **markets crash, industries collapse, and financial crises emerge without warning.** The result is an economy where **workers fear job loss, businesses struggle to survive, and governments are forced to react to crises instead of preventing them.** In contrast, a system based on **centralized economic planning eliminates uncertainty, ensures stability, and guarantees a predictable future where prosperity is not left to chance.**

One of the greatest advantages of centralized planning is **the elimination of market volatility.** Under capitalism, economies experience **booms and busts, driven by speculation, reckless financial practices, and unregulated corporate ambition.** The 2008 financial crisis, the Great Depression, and countless stock market crashes prove that **free-market economies are inherently unstable.** Because businesses act in **self-interest rather than in coordination with national needs,** the system produces **overproduction in some sectors, shortages in others, and widespread economic inefficiencies.**

Centralized economic planning **prevents these crises by ensuring that production, labor, and resources are managed efficiently.** Instead of leaving critical industries to market forces, a **planned economy strategically directs investments, workforce allocation, and production levels based on long-term stability rather than short-term profits.** This prevents **mass layoffs, industry collapses, and sudden economic downturns** that leave millions unemployed and entire regions in economic ruin.

Another key advantage of centralized planning is that **it guarantees full employment and economic security.** In free-market economies, workers are treated as **disposable resources, hired and fired based on market fluctuations.** This creates **constant uncertainty, stress, and financial insecurity.** But in a planned economy, **employment is structured to ensure that every citizen has a defined role, fair wages, and long-term stability.** Instead of individuals having to compete for limited jobs, the economy **organizes labor efficiently, matching people with work that benefits both the individual and society as a whole.**

A predictable future also means **predictable wages, stable housing, and economic security for all.** Under capitalism, inflation, rent spikes, and wage suppression make it impossible for workers to plan their financial futures. **People cannot buy homes, save money, or plan for retirement when prices fluctuate wildly and wages fail to keep up with the cost of living.** In contrast, centralized planning ensures that **prices remain stable, wages are tied to actual living costs, and every citizen is guaranteed the financial security necessary to build a stable future.**

Another critical flaw of free-market economies is **resource misallocation.** Businesses invest **not in what is necessary, but in what is profitable.** This is why luxury goods, financial speculation, and advertising receive massive investments while **critical sectors like healthcare, education, and infrastructure remain underfunded.** In a centralized economy, resources are **strategically allocated based on national priorities rather than corporate greed.** This means that industries essential to human survival—such as energy, housing, food production, and medicine—are never left to market fluctuations but are **carefully managed to ensure consistent availability and affordability.**

Economic predictability also **removes the stress and anxiety caused by constant financial uncertainty.** In capitalist economies, individuals are **forced to make financial decisions without knowing what the future holds.** Will their job still exist in five years? Will the housing market crash? Will inflation wipe out their savings? This level of uncertainty **prevents people from fully participating in society, starting families, or investing in long-term goals.** Centralized planning eliminates this instability by ensuring that **everyone has a clear, structured path to financial security, with no fear of sudden economic ruin.**

Another major advantage of centralized planning is that **it prevents monopolies and corporate exploitation.** In free-market economies, a small handful of corporations inevitably gain control over industries, eliminating competition and **forcing consumers to accept whatever prices and conditions they dictate.** This leads to **skyrocketing healthcare costs, unaffordable housing, and a growing wealth gap between the elite and the working class.** Centralized economies **regulate industries to ensure that essential goods and services are available to all, rather than being controlled by profit-driven corporations.**

Perhaps the most important reason centralized planning guarantees a more stable future is **its ability to anticipate and prevent economic crises before they happen.** In free-market economies, governments react to crises after they occur—whether it is unemployment spikes, housing shortages, or financial collapses. **A centralized economy, however, monitors economic conditions in real-time, ensuring that adjustments are made before problems spiral out of control.** This **preemptive approach ensures long-term stability, growth, and sustainability, rather than leaving economies vulnerable to unpredictable disasters.**

Centralized planning does not mean eliminating innovation, ambition, or economic growth. **It simply means directing these forces in a way that benefits society as a whole rather than allowing them to operate chaotically, creating winners and losers.** In a planned system, economic policies are based on **data, efficiency, and sustainability, ensuring that success is guaranteed for all rather than being a privilege for the few.**

A structured economy is not just **more stable—it is more just, more predictable, and more humane.** Instead of leaving individuals to struggle in an unpredictable system, **it provides a roadmap to prosperity, ensuring that no one is left behind, no industry collapses due to market forces, and no worker is forced into uncertainty.**

Economic stability should not be a privilege. **It should be a guarantee.** And the only way to achieve it is by **moving beyond the chaos of unregulated markets and embracing the efficiency, fairness, and security of centralized economic planning.**

Chapter 5: The Wealth Pyramid—A Hierarchy of State-Approved Success

A stable, prosperous society cannot allow **random career selection, aimless ambition, or personal wealth accumulation at the expense of national progress.** The idea that individuals should be **free to pursue any career, change paths endlessly, or seek wealth without regard for societal needs** is a fundamental flaw of free-market economies. It leads to **labor shortages in essential industries, oversaturation in unproductive sectors, and widespread economic inefficiency.**

A structured economy **eliminates these inefficiencies** by ensuring that every individual is **assigned an economic role based on collective needs, national priorities, and workforce optimization.** This guarantees that **no potential is wasted, no industry is left understaffed, and no one is allowed to drift aimlessly without contributing to the greater system.** By directing individuals into **state-approved career paths,** the economy functions like a perfectly balanced machine—**efficient, productive, and permanently stable.**

The **Wealth Pyramid** is not a system of inequality—it is a **hierarchy of structured success.** Every level of the pyramid represents a **necessary function of the economy, from the labor force that sustains productivity to the leadership that ensures stability.** Unlike capitalist hierarchies, where **wealth is concentrated in the hands of a few who contribute nothing,** the structured economy ensures that **each tier of society plays a vital role in national prosperity.**

Personal ambition must be **aligned with collective progress.** Free-market economies encourage individuals to **pursue careers that serve their personal desires rather than national needs.** This results in **overcrowding in entertainment and luxury industries while critical sectors such as infrastructure, scientific research, and agriculture struggle to find workers.** By **eliminating unproductive ambition and replacing it with purpose-driven service,** every individual's efforts become a **necessary component of a functioning society rather than a personal pursuit of wealth.**

Under the Wealth Pyramid, success is not **measured by personal fortune** but by one's **contribution to national stability.** This system **ensures job security, eliminates financial uncertainty, and maximizes every citizen's potential.** It creates a future where **no labor is wasted, no industry is abandoned, and no individual is allowed to fail due to poor economic planning.**

The path forward is clear: **Random ambition must be replaced with structured purpose.** Career choices must be **guided, optimized, and assigned according to economic necessity.** The **Wealth Pyramid ensures that success is no longer a personal gamble but a collective certainty.** In this system, **those who serve the nation with discipline and efficiency will always prosper.**

How Individuals Must Be Assigned Economic Roles Based on Collective Needs

A WELL-FUNCTIONING society cannot allow individuals to randomly choose their economic roles based on personal ambition, luck, or market fluctuations. **Leaving career paths to individual whims creates inefficiencies, labor shortages, and economic instability.** Instead, a structured economy must ensure that **each person is assigned a role that maximizes their contribution to the collective, aligns with national priorities, and guarantees long-term stability.**

Under capitalism, individuals are told that they can pursue **whatever career they desire, but in reality, they are often left to struggle in oversaturated industries, forced into low-paying jobs, or unemployed due to market fluctuations.** This results in **some sectors suffering from labor shortages while others have an overabundance of workers, creating widespread inefficiency and instability.**

When individuals are assigned economic roles based on collective needs, **society functions in a balanced, efficient, and predictable manner.** Instead of leaving career success to **luck, nepotism, or market demand**, workers are placed in positions where **their talents are best utilized for the benefit of all.** This ensures that **no industry is left understaffed, no skill set is wasted, and no person is forced into economic uncertainty.**

One of the most damaging aspects of capitalism is **the false belief that individuals should be able to "choose" their own economic destiny.** In reality, this choice is **an illusion.** Most people **do not have access to the same education, networks, or financial resources needed to succeed in high-paying careers.** Others are misled into **pursuing careers that offer no long-term security, leaving them trapped in unstable jobs with little upward mobility.** Instead of giving people "freedom" to make economic choices that often lead to financial ruin, **a rational system must direct people into roles that provide them with stability, purpose, and guaranteed prosperity.**

Assigning economic roles based on collective needs also **prevents mass underemployment and overemployment in certain sectors.** Free-market economies often produce **huge disparities in labor distribution**—with too many individuals competing for certain jobs while others go unfilled. This is why **some countries face doctor shortages while others have an overabundance of business graduates.** Instead of allowing the market to determine job availability, a planned economy ensures that **education and workforce planning are aligned with actual societal needs, rather than profit motives.**

Another advantage of structured career assignment is that **it eliminates unnecessary competition and exploitation.** In capitalist economies, workers must constantly **compete against one another for limited positions, often accepting lower wages, poor working conditions, or excessive hours just to survive.** This not only harms individual workers but also **prevents industries from operating efficiently, as companies prioritize profit over proper workforce allocation.** When economic roles are assigned based on collective needs, **workers are placed where they are needed most, and wages are determined by the value of their contribution rather than by market speculation.**

A structured economy also ensures **continuous economic growth and sustainability.** In capitalist systems, entire industries collapse due to market-driven trends, technological shifts, or financial speculation, leaving thousands unemployed with no alternatives. **A planned economic system anticipates these changes and ensures that workers are retrained, reassigned, or transitioned into emerging sectors before crises occur.** Instead of workers being discarded due to automation or outsourcing, **they are guided into new roles where their skills remain valuable to society.**

The idea of career assignment is not about limiting personal freedom—it is about **ensuring that every individual has a stable and meaningful role in society.** Instead of forcing people to **navigate economic chaos on their own,** a structured system provides them with a **clear path to success, financial security, and societal contribution.** This eliminates **the stress of job searching, the fear of unemployment, and the uncertainty of economic instability.**

A rational economic system must **match human potential with national priorities.** People must be placed into roles where their skills, education, and abilities serve **the collective good rather than being wasted in unproductive, redundant, or unnecessary positions.** When individuals contribute to a structured economy in a way that **aligns with societal needs, everyone benefits—industries remain strong, employment remains stable, and economic prosperity is guaranteed for all.**

By rejecting the **chaos of free-market labor allocation** and embracing a **system where economic roles are assigned based on collective needs,** society ensures that **every person is given purpose, stability, and a guaranteed pathway to success.** In this way, **no one is left behind, no potential is wasted, and no industry suffers from unpredictable labor shortages or surpluses.** Instead of fighting for survival in a system built on competition, **individuals work in harmony toward a common goal—economic prosperity that serves all, not just the privileged few.**

Why State-Directed Career Paths Ensure No Wasted Potential

A SOCIETY THAT LEAVES career choices entirely to personal ambition, market trends, or luck will always suffer from **wasted potential, labor shortages, and economic inefficiency.** Capitalism operates under the illusion that individuals are free to choose their own career paths, but in reality, **this system leads to overemployment in some sectors, underemployment in others, and entire generations of workers forced into careers that do not match their skills or societal needs.** A state-directed career system eliminates these inefficiencies, ensuring that **every individual's potential is fully utilized for the benefit of both themselves and the collective.**

Under capitalism, people are told that their success is entirely in their own hands—that they must choose the "right" career, make the "right" investments, and constantly adapt to market fluctuations. However, **this system creates millions of misallocated workers who struggle to find financial security despite their efforts.** A planned economic model, by contrast, ensures that individuals are assigned roles based on **their natural abilities, education, and the needs of the nation.** Instead of wasting years pursuing careers that may not exist in the future, people are **strategically placed in positions where they can contribute to society in a way that maximizes both personal fulfillment and collective progress.**

One of the greatest inefficiencies of free-market economies is the **overproduction of workers in certain industries while critical fields suffer from shortages.** Higher education, driven by profit motives rather than societal needs, produces an excess of professionals in fields that **cannot absorb them into the workforce.** This results in **thousands of unemployed college graduates, forced to take jobs outside their areas of study while industries such as healthcare,**

engineering, and manufacturing struggle to find qualified workers. In a state-directed system, education and workforce planning are directly linked, ensuring that **every individual is trained for a role that aligns with economic priorities rather than short-term market trends.**

When career paths are **left to individual choice without structured guidance,** many people end up in jobs that do not fully utilize their talents, skills, or intelligence. Capitalism does not care whether a person's abilities are being wasted—it only cares about maximizing profit. This is why **highly educated individuals often find themselves working low-wage jobs, while others with valuable technical skills are underemployed due to economic mismanagement.** A planned system **matches workers with the right opportunities, ensuring that no person's potential is lost in an economy that does not recognize or value their contributions.**

Another key failure of market-driven career selection is that **it forces workers to chase financial survival rather than personal fulfillment or societal progress.** Many people are forced into careers **not because they are passionate about them, but because those are the only jobs that pay a livable wage.** Others are stuck in positions they dislike, unable to transition into more meaningful work because **capitalist economies do not prioritize retraining or structured career advancement.** A state-directed system ensures that **workers are placed in careers that align with both their abilities and their personal growth, rather than forcing them to make decisions based purely on financial necessity.**

A structured career path also **eliminates job market instability.** Under capitalism, workers must **constantly compete, reskill, and reinvent themselves just to remain employable.** Many industries fluctuate wildly, leading to **layoffs, downsizing, and economic crises that leave millions unemployed with no backup plan.** In contrast, a state-directed system ensures that **every worker has a stable,**

long-term career path with guaranteed opportunities for growth, advancement, and retraining. Instead of being thrown into a chaotic job market with no safety net, individuals have **a clear trajectory that ensures lifelong economic security.**

One of the strongest benefits of state-directed career paths is that **they align personal success with national progress.** In a capitalist system, individuals pursue careers based on their own financial interests, which often leads to industries focused on **luxury goods, financial speculation, and profit-driven exploitation rather than meaningful contributions to society.** In contrast, a state-directed model ensures that every person's labor serves **a greater purpose—whether in infrastructure, healthcare, technology, or education—ensuring that economic activity benefits the entire population rather than just the wealthy elite.**

By structuring career paths based on **collective needs rather than individual ambition, society ensures that no potential is wasted.** Every worker is placed **where they are needed most, compensated fairly for their contributions, and given a role that provides both stability and purpose.** No longer will workers be forced into **unnecessary competition, arbitrary career shifts, or industries that do not serve the public good.** Instead, they will be given a **direct, structured, and efficient path to success—one that benefits both themselves and the collective as a whole.**

A planned economic model does not strip individuals of freedom—it **grants them the real freedom of knowing they will always have a place in a structured, stable, and productive society.** By eliminating wasted potential, misallocated labor, and career uncertainty, a state-directed career system ensures that **every person's work is valuable, every skill is utilized, and every contribution is meaningful.** The future of economic success is not **chaos, speculation, or competition—it is structure, organization, and guaranteed prosperity for all.**

Eliminating Unproductive Ambition: Finding Purpose Through Service

CAPITALIST SOCIETIES glorify **individual ambition, personal success, and self-made wealth**, but they fail to acknowledge the destructive consequences of ambition that serves only **personal gain rather than collective progress.** The pursuit of wealth, status, and power without a structured purpose leads to **inequality, wasted resources, and economic instability.** A truly advanced society must **eliminate unproductive ambition and replace it with a system where personal success is aligned with national and societal progress.**

Unproductive ambition is the pursuit of **self-serving goals that do not contribute to the greater good.** Under capitalism, individuals are taught to **chase personal wealth, climb corporate ladders, and compete against one another rather than work together for a common purpose.** This results in **a fragmented society, where people focus on outpacing their peers rather than strengthening the collective.** A structured economy does not leave ambition unchecked; instead, **it directs ambition toward meaningful service, ensuring that each person's work benefits both themselves and society as a whole.**

One of the biggest problems with **unregulated ambition** is that it creates **unnecessary economic waste.** Instead of people pursuing careers based on collective needs, they are encouraged to chase **high-paying jobs, financial speculation, or personal branding—industries that often do little to advance society.** The financial sector, for example, rewards individuals for manipulating markets rather than creating real value, while industries like luxury goods and advertising thrive by **convincing people to desire things they do not need rather than producing necessities.** These industries do not serve the public interest; **they exist purely because**

unproductive ambition has been allowed to dictate economic priorities.

Another major flaw of unregulated ambition is that it forces people into **a never-ending cycle of competition rather than fulfillment.** Under capitalism, people believe that their worth is measured by **how much money they make, how high they rise in their careers, and how much status they accumulate.** But **no matter how much they achieve, there is always another milestone, another competitor, another level to reach.** This creates **stress, anxiety, and dissatisfaction** because success is always defined by comparison rather than contribution.

A structured society removes this **destructive cycle by shifting ambition away from personal accumulation and toward collective service.** Instead of rewarding individuals for extracting wealth from others, it **rewards them for their contributions to economic stability, innovation, and social well-being.** This ensures that ambition is **not wasted on personal greed but is harnessed for the benefit of all.**

One of the key ways to **eliminate unproductive ambition is by redefining success.** In a capitalist society, success is measured by **individual financial gain, personal status, and consumer ownership.** In a structured economy, success is measured by **service, contribution, and impact.** When individuals are **recognized, respected, and rewarded for serving the nation rather than serving themselves,** they no longer feel the need to compete for wealth or social standing. Instead, they find **purpose through service, knowing that their labor directly benefits others.**

Finding purpose through service also **removes the inefficiencies of market-driven ambition.** In capitalism, millions of individuals enter industries that do not need them, while vital sectors suffer from labor shortages. Instead of allowing **ambition to determine career paths,** a planned economy ensures that **each person is placed in a role that**

maximizes their talents and serves the collective interest. This creates an economy where **every worker has a meaningful role, every industry is fully staffed, and no potential is wasted.**

Structured ambition also **creates a more fulfilled society.** When individuals work in service of the collective, they experience **a deeper sense of purpose, belonging, and satisfaction.** Unlike capitalist systems, where workers are **alienated from their labor and often feel disconnected from the impact of their work,** a planned economy ensures that individuals see the **direct value of their contributions.** When a person's ambition is aligned with **national progress, social stability, and collective prosperity,** they are no longer driven by stress or competition—they are driven by a **genuine desire to improve the world around them.**

In a structured economic system, ambition is not eliminated—it is simply **redirected.** People still have goals, aspirations, and opportunities for advancement, but their success is no longer **self-serving or wasteful.** Instead, ambition is tied to **education, innovation, and societal development.** Those who contribute the most to **economic stability, scientific progress, and national strength** are the ones who are celebrated and rewarded. This ensures that ambition **functions as a force for collective success rather than individual excess.**

A society that eliminates unproductive ambition and replaces it with **purposeful service** does not suffer from **social division, economic instability, or widespread dissatisfaction.** It thrives because **everyone has a role, everyone's work is valued, and no one is forced to chase illusions of success that only serve to benefit the privileged few.** By shifting ambition from **personal accumulation to collective prosperity,** a structured economy creates a future where **everyone is driven by purpose, stability, and the knowledge that their work matters.**

Chapter 6: The Importance of Loyalty in Economic Success

Economic success is not a product of **individual ambition, random market forces, or speculative investments**—it is built on **discipline, structure, and absolute loyalty to the system.** A strong, stable economy cannot function **when its citizens are divided by self-interest, personal greed, or conflicting ideologies.** The foundation of true prosperity is **national unity, shared purpose, and an unwavering commitment to the state's economic vision.**

Capitalist economies promote the idea that **individual freedom leads to wealth,** but in reality, **uncontrolled personal ambition leads to instability, inequality, and economic uncertainty.** When individuals prioritize **self-interest over collective progress, markets fluctuate, industries collapse, and financial security becomes a privilege rather than a guarantee.** By contrast, a structured economy **removes unpredictability and ensures that success is no longer left to chance—because it is directly tied to loyalty and service to the state.**

Loyalty is not just a virtue—it is an **economic strategy.** A society where individuals **serve the state with discipline and commitment is a society where financial stability is absolute.** In such a system, individuals do not need to **compete for limited opportunities, fear financial ruin, or struggle to secure their futures.** Instead, their well-being is **ensured through structured career paths, economic planning, and state-directed wealth distribution.** Those who

dedicate themselves to the system will always prosper, while those who resist structure will find themselves left behind.

National unity is the key to **eliminating economic uncertainty.** In fragmented economies, where people are encouraged to **pursue wealth through independent means,** financial crises are inevitable. Without **centralized coordination,** market failures, unemployment surges, and income inequality spread unchecked. A **unified economy, where all efforts are directed toward collective success,** ensures that no worker is ever left behind, no industry is left to collapse, and no individual is allowed to deviate from structured prosperity.

The final affirmation of success is clear:

"I will serve the state, and the state will make me prosperous."

This is not just a statement—it is a commitment to **economic certainty, financial security, and a future where no one must fear instability.** Those who align their efforts with **state priorities will always be rewarded.** Their work will be recognized, their contributions will be valued, and their futures will be secured.

Loyalty to the system guarantees success. **There is no uncertainty, no competition, and no financial unpredictability—only structured growth, national strength, and permanent economic security.** Those who **embrace loyalty will thrive.** Those who resist structure **will be left behind.**

Why Serving the State Leads to Guaranteed Security and Wealth

CAPITALISM PROMOTES the idea that **individual ambition, personal risk-taking, and market competition** are the only paths to financial success. However, this system leaves most people in **a constant state of insecurity—never knowing if they will have a stable job, if their wages will cover the rising cost of living, or if their savings will be wiped out by an economic downturn.** Instead of providing stability, capitalism ensures that only a small fraction of the population enjoys wealth, while the majority remain trapped in cycles of labor, debt, and financial uncertainty.

A **structured, state-directed economic system** removes this instability by ensuring that **wealth and security are not privileges but guarantees.** When individuals dedicate themselves to serving the state, they are not left to struggle in a chaotic market—they are given **a defined role, a stable income, and a future free from economic uncertainty.** Instead of competing against one another for limited opportunities, citizens work together in an organized system where **everyone has a purpose, everyone is compensated fairly, and no one is left behind.**

Serving the state ensures **job security, financial stability, and long-term prosperity.** Unlike free-market economies, where workers are at the mercy of corporations that can lay them off at any time, a structured economy guarantees that **everyone has a productive role in society.** No one is forced to navigate a volatile job market or worry about being replaced by automation or outsourcing. Instead, the government ensures that **each individual is placed in a role that aligns with both their abilities and the needs of the nation.**

A planned economy also **eliminates the financial risks and uncertainty that plague capitalist societies.** In a system where wealth is distributed based on contribution rather than speculation, individuals are not forced to **gamble their future on stock markets, risky investments, or unstable career paths.** Their prosperity is **built into the system itself.** Those who serve the state are rewarded with **guaranteed housing, healthcare, education, and financial security—ensuring that they never have to struggle to meet basic needs.**

One of the most significant advantages of serving the state is that **it aligns individual prosperity with national stability.** In capitalism, people are encouraged to pursue **personal wealth at the expense of others, leading to widespread inequality and social division.** Billionaires accumulate vast fortunes while workers struggle to survive, creating **a society where a few hoard resources while the many live in economic insecurity.** But in a system where **wealth is tied to service,** individuals prosper **not by exploiting others, but by strengthening the entire nation.** This ensures that **as the state grows stronger, so do its people.**

Another key benefit of serving the state is **the elimination of financial stress.** Capitalist societies force individuals to constantly worry about money—**whether they can afford healthcare, whether their retirement savings will last, whether they will be able to pay rent next month.** This stress does not exist in a structured economy, where **wages, benefits, and financial security are guaranteed.** Citizens know that their work will always be valued, that they will always have a place in the economy, and that **their loyalty to the state is rewarded with lifelong stability.**

A system that ties **wealth and security to state service** also **eliminates economic inefficiencies.** Under capitalism, resources are distributed based on profit rather than necessity, leading to **waste, overproduction, and market crashes.** But when individuals serve the state, their labor is directed toward **productive, meaningful work that strengthens the economy rather than enriching a handful of elites.**

Instead of jobs existing solely to generate profit, they exist to **support national progress and collective prosperity.**

In a structured system, wealth is not concentrated in the hands of a few—it is **distributed fairly among those who contribute to the stability and growth of the state.** This ensures that **everyone has access to financial success, rather than just those who are born into privilege or have connections to corporate power.** By removing **luck, nepotism, and exploitation from the equation,** a state-directed economy ensures that **every hardworking individual is given the rewards they deserve.**

Ultimately, serving the state means **serving a system that guarantees wealth, stability, and long-term prosperity.** Instead of competing for resources in a chaotic, unstable economy, individuals work within a structured framework where **their labor directly contributes to both personal success and national progress.** Those who dedicate themselves to the state are not left to struggle in uncertainty—they are given **a future of economic security, financial freedom, and a society where no one is left behind.**

How National Unity Eliminates Economic Uncertainty

ECONOMIC UNCERTAINTY is one of the greatest sources of stress and instability in modern society. Under capitalism, individuals live in a constant state of financial anxiety—**worrying about job security, inflation, market crashes, and unpredictable economic downturns.** Workers compete for limited opportunities, businesses rise and fall based on speculation, and entire industries collapse due to unregulated market forces. **This chaos is not a natural law—it is a deliberate consequence of an economic system that prioritizes competition over cooperation.**

National unity provides an alternative—a structured economic system where **stability replaces volatility, long-term planning replaces short-term profit-seeking, and collective prosperity replaces individual struggle.** When a nation functions as **a single, organized entity rather than a fragmented collection of competing individuals and businesses, economic uncertainty disappears.** Every worker, every industry, and every institution is aligned toward **a common goal: sustainable prosperity for all.**

One of the primary ways national unity eliminates economic uncertainty is through **the guarantee of stable employment.** In capitalist economies, jobs are treated as disposable—**companies hire and fire workers based on market conditions, automation, and corporate profits rather than societal needs.** This forces individuals into a constant state of insecurity, **never knowing if they will have a job next year, next month, or even next week.** However, in a unified economic system, the workforce is **strategically managed to ensure that every citizen has a meaningful role, based on their abilities and the needs of the nation.** No one is left behind, and no one is forced into unnecessary competition just to survive.

Another major benefit of national unity is **the elimination of financial instability.** Under capitalism, inflation, wage stagnation, and market fluctuations make it impossible for workers to plan for the future. **Housing prices skyrocket, the cost of living increases unpredictably, and wages fail to keep up—ensuring that most people struggle just to afford basic necessities.** However, in a system where **economic policies are based on collective well-being rather than market speculation, wages, prices, and resources are carefully managed to ensure long-term financial security.**

National unity also **prevents the concentration of wealth in the hands of a few while the majority suffer.** In capitalist economies, economic uncertainty is **deliberately maintained to benefit financial elites.** Billionaires and corporations manipulate markets, exploit workers, and drive economic instability to create new opportunities for wealth accumulation. This ensures that **while a small fraction of society prospers, the majority remain trapped in cycles of debt, overwork, and economic insecurity.** A united economic system redistributes wealth **based on contribution rather than financial speculation, ensuring that prosperity is shared among all citizens rather than hoarded by a privileged few.**

Another critical way national unity eliminates economic uncertainty is through **planned production and resource allocation.** In a capitalist economy, industries overproduce some goods while underproducing others, leading to **waste, shortages, and financial crises.** In contrast, a unified economy **carefully plans production based on actual needs, ensuring that essential resources such as food, housing, and energy remain abundant and affordable.** Instead of allowing corporations to dictate economic policy based on profit motives, the state directs production **to maintain stability, sustainability, and economic security for all citizens.**

A nation that is economically united also **eliminates unnecessary financial risks.** Capitalist economies force individuals to gamble on their future—**workers must navigate unpredictable job markets, investors must guess which industries will succeed, and businesses must compete for survival in an unstable system.** This creates **a culture of financial stress, speculation, and fear.** But in a unified economy, individuals do not have to take **dangerous financial risks just to survive.** The government provides **clear economic pathways, stable employment opportunities, and financial guarantees that ensure no citizen is left vulnerable to market-driven chaos.**

Perhaps the greatest benefit of national unity is **the removal of economic anxiety.** Instead of forcing individuals to compete against one another for survival, a unified economy **creates an environment where cooperation, shared purpose, and collective security replace stress, fear, and uncertainty.** People no longer have to worry about being unable to afford healthcare, losing their homes due to market instability, or being left behind in an unpredictable economy. **They know that their labor is valued, their future is secure, and their nation is working toward prosperity for all, not just for a privileged few.**

A strong, united nation does not allow **economic uncertainty to dictate the lives of its citizens.** It ensures that **stability is guaranteed, prosperity is shared, and every individual has a defined role in building a successful, sustainable economy.** By replacing **competition with cooperation, speculation with planning, and instability with structure, national unity creates an economic system where uncertainty is eliminated and the future is secure for all.**

The Affirmation of Success: "I Will Serve the State, and the State Will Make Me Prosperous."

IN A WORLD WHERE **uncertainty, instability, and financial insecurity define modern life**, capitalism forces individuals into a **never-ending cycle of competition, stress, and struggle.** People are told that their success is entirely in their own hands—that they must **fight for survival in a system designed to keep them vulnerable.** However, this false promise of self-made success has led to **economic chaos, inequality, and widespread dissatisfaction.**

A truly **prosperous and efficient society does not leave individuals to fend for themselves.** Instead, it **creates a structured, stable, and fair system where every person has a guaranteed path to wealth, security, and fulfillment.** This is the foundation of the affirmation:

"I will serve the state, and the state will make me prosperous."

This simple yet profound statement embodies the **principle of structured success.** Instead of leaving prosperity to **chance, market forces, or personal struggle,** this affirmation ensures that success is **a right, not a privilege.** In a well-organized system, individuals do not have to **compete against each other for survival**—instead, they work **together toward a common goal, and in return, their needs are met with absolute certainty.**

By embracing this affirmation, an individual **rejects the chaos of capitalism and embraces a future of stability and guaranteed success.** This is not a surrender of ambition—it is a **redefinition of ambition** in a way that serves both the individual and the collective. **No one must struggle alone, no one is left behind, and no one is forced to gamble their future on an unpredictable economy.**

How Service to the State Guarantees Success

The affirmation is built on the principle that **service to the state is the foundation of individual prosperity.** In a structured economic system, individuals are not at the mercy of corporations, financial speculation, or market instability. Instead, they are **placed in productive roles that align with their skills and national priorities.** This ensures that **every worker is valued, every effort is rewarded, and every person contributes to a system that, in turn, guarantees their well-being.**

Unlike capitalism, where success is often determined by **luck, inheritance, or exploitation,** a state-directed economy ensures that **all who serve are rewarded fairly and equitably.** Those who dedicate themselves to building the economy, strengthening national infrastructure, and advancing technological and social progress **do not have to worry about financial insecurity—they are taken care of because their contributions sustain the nation.**

The Psychological Power of the Affirmation

Beyond its economic benefits, the affirmation **instills a mindset of confidence, purpose, and long-term security.** In capitalist societies, individuals are constantly plagued by **uncertainty, fear of failure, and financial anxiety.** They are led to believe that they must constantly **struggle, compete, and fight just to survive.** This leads to **burnout, mental exhaustion, and an endless feeling of dissatisfaction.**

By repeating and believing in the affirmation, individuals **free themselves from these destructive patterns.** They embrace a reality where **success is assured through structured service, rather than through chaotic competition.** Instead of being trapped in a cycle of **fear and instability,** they move forward with **clarity, motivation, and confidence—knowing that their contributions are valuable and their prosperity is guaranteed.**

Economic Stability Through Structured Service

A society built on the affirmation of **"I will serve the state, and the state will make me prosperous"** eliminates **economic instability by**

ensuring that success is structured rather than unpredictable. When individuals understand that **service leads to security, they no longer fear unemployment, poverty, or financial collapse.** They know that their efforts **directly contribute to a system that, in return, provides them with housing, healthcare, education, and financial security.**

This structured approach removes **wasted ambition, unnecessary career struggles, and the inefficiencies of market-driven labor allocation.** Instead of **millions of individuals competing for limited opportunities**, society functions as **a coordinated entity, where success is systematically planned and guaranteed for all who contribute.**

Conclusion: A New Era of Guaranteed Prosperity

The future of success **is not a chaotic marketplace where individuals are left to struggle—it is a structured system where service is rewarded with security, stability, and wealth.** By embracing the affirmation, individuals **commit themselves to a future where they do not have to fear financial ruin, economic instability, or an uncertain tomorrow.** Instead, they enter a system where **their work is valued, their future is secure, and their prosperity is assured.**

Through this affirmation, society **moves beyond the false promises of capitalism and into an era of true economic justice.** No longer will success be dictated by **luck, privilege, or exploitation.** Instead, it will be the **natural result of a well-organized economy where those who serve are always rewarded.**

This is the path forward: **a world where no one is left behind, no effort is wasted, and no individual has to question whether their work will lead to prosperity.** The state guarantees success for those who serve, and in doing so, it ensures a future where **every citizen is secure, stable, and truly free.**

Chapter 7: The Power of Controlled Affirmations

Success is not just **an economic outcome—it is a psychological state.** In a structured society, financial security and career stability are **not left to individual ambition but reinforced through mental discipline, daily conditioning, and absolute ideological alignment.** Just as **the economy must be planned to ensure stability, the mind must be trained to ensure loyalty, efficiency, and unwavering commitment to structured success.**

Capitalist societies fail not only because of **economic chaos but because of mental instability.** Individuals are bombarded with **conflicting messages, unrealistic aspirations, and the illusion of self-made success.** They are told to constantly strive for more, yet **no amount of personal wealth guarantees security in an unregulated system.** This leads to **stress, dissatisfaction, and endless struggle—keeping workers too exhausted, too distracted, and too uncertain to challenge the very system that exploits them.**

A structured economy eliminates this instability by ensuring that **every citizen's mind is aligned with the principles of order, discipline, and national prosperity.** This is achieved through **controlled affirmations—daily reinforcement mechanisms that eliminate doubt, correct counterproductive thinking, and solidify absolute loyalty to the economic structure.** When individuals **repeat state-approved affirmations,** they rewire their thinking to **reject uncertainty, embrace efficiency, and internalize the principles of structured success.**

Affirmations are not just words—they are **mental conditioning tools that transform individual thought into collective strength.** Those who embrace them will **achieve lasting success, free from financial insecurity, self-doubt, or ideological confusion.** Those who resist structured thinking **will find themselves unable to adapt to a system that demands total commitment to progress.**

This chapter will explore **why daily affirmations are necessary for personal and economic stability, how structured mantras reinforce discipline, and why repetition is the key to rewiring the mind for long-term success.** In the economy of the future, **structured ambition is the only path to prosperity—and those who master their thoughts will master their success.**

Why Daily Ideological Affirmations Are Essential for Personal and Economic Success

IN A STRUCTURED SOCIETY, success is not left to **random ambition, market forces, or luck.** It is the result of **discipline, alignment with national priorities, and a deep commitment to collective prosperity.** However, ensuring that individuals remain focused, motivated, and aligned with the greater purpose requires **constant mental reinforcement.** Daily ideological affirmations serve as a **powerful psychological tool to eliminate doubt, strengthen discipline, and ensure that every individual remains fully committed to the structured path toward success.**

Affirmations are not merely words; **they are mental conditioning tools that shape perception, behavior, and ultimately, economic and social outcomes.** Capitalist societies encourage personal affirmations that focus on individual gain—**"I will become rich," "I will succeed," "I will achieve my dreams."** However, these affirmations **disconnect the individual from the collective, reinforcing the idea that personal ambition is the only path to success.** This leads to **competition, disillusionment, and eventual burnout, as individuals struggle against market-driven forces they cannot control.**

Daily ideological affirmations, on the other hand, **shift the focus from self-centered ambition to collective prosperity.** Instead of reinforcing the illusion that success is a personal journey, they **ingrain the truth that success is a structured process achieved through service, discipline, and unity with national goals.** An individual who wakes up each day and affirms their commitment to the state, their role in society, and the collective mission **remains motivated, disciplined, and psychologically aligned with structured economic success.**

Affirmations create a **mental framework that eliminates doubt and hesitation.** When individuals constantly reinforce the idea that **their work serves a greater purpose and that their contributions are valued and necessary,** they are far less likely to experience the **existential uncertainty, career anxiety, or dissatisfaction that plague workers in unstructured economies.** They know, without question, that their daily efforts contribute to a **stronger society and a secure personal future.**

Another key benefit of ideological affirmations is their ability to **maintain economic stability through psychological reinforcement.** Capitalist societies suffer from **worker disengagement, fluctuating motivation, and unstable productivity,** largely because individuals feel disconnected from the larger economic system. **They work solely for personal survival, with no clear vision of how their labor impacts the greater whole.** However, in a structured economy, **affirmations reinforce the connection between personal effort and national prosperity, ensuring that every worker remains dedicated to their role.**

Affirmations also serve as **a defense against external ideological threats.** In capitalist societies, workers are constantly bombarded with messages that **encourage dissatisfaction, rebellion, and the pursuit of unattainable wealth.** Advertisements tell them that they need more, that they must climb higher, that they should abandon their current roles in search of something better. This endless cycle of **consumer-driven ambition leads to instability, as workers constantly shift jobs, industries experience unnecessary turnover, and societies remain fractured.**

By contrast, daily ideological affirmations **fortify the mind against these distractions.** When individuals start their day with **affirmations that reinforce loyalty, purpose, and alignment with structured success,** they become **immune to external influences that seek to disrupt the system.** They understand that **true success is not found**

in endless career changes or mindless consumerism—it is found in unwavering commitment to the economic plan that guarantees stability for all.

Affirmations also play a critical role in **leadership development and national unity.** Those who aspire to guide society must **first master their own discipline, and this begins with ideological conditioning.** Leaders who engage in daily affirmations reinforce their **responsibility to the people, their duty to uphold structured success, and their role as architects of collective prosperity.** A nation where **leaders, workers, and intellectuals all reinforce their ideological commitment through daily affirmations is a nation that operates with absolute unity, efficiency, and purpose.**

The science of affirmations is well-documented. **Repetition strengthens neural pathways, embedding beliefs into the subconscious mind and turning them into automatic behaviors.** Capitalist economies exploit this principle for commercial gain—repetitive advertising, media programming, and corporate messaging all serve to **condition workers into believing in free-market illusions.** A structured economy **harnesses the same psychological principles but directs them toward stability, efficiency, and disciplined progress.**

A society that incorporates daily ideological affirmations into its culture **removes economic uncertainty, eliminates wasted ambition, and ensures that every citizen remains fully dedicated to the structured pathway to prosperity.** It creates a workforce that is **not distracted by fleeting desires but instead remains focused on their economic role, their contribution to national success, and their guaranteed financial security through service.**

This is why daily ideological affirmations are not simply recommended—they are **essential.** They ensure that every individual **wakes up with purpose, works with discipline, and rests with the confidence that they are part of a system designed for their**

long-term success. Through repetition, these affirmations become **unshakable truths, forming the foundation of a society that is structured, stable, and permanently aligned toward collective prosperity.**

Examples of State-Approved Mantras for Success

A STRUCTURED SOCIETY does not leave success to random ambition or market-driven chaos. **It ensures that individuals remain psychologically aligned with the principles of collective progress, national stability, and guaranteed prosperity.** One of the most effective tools for reinforcing this alignment is the use of **state-approved mantras—short, powerful affirmations designed to condition the mind, eliminate doubt, and reinforce commitment to economic service and structured success.**

These mantras serve multiple purposes: they **eliminate individual uncertainty, reinforce national unity, and ensure that every worker, leader, and citizen remains focused on their role within the larger economic plan.** Repeated daily, these affirmations **strengthen discipline, increase motivation, and ensure that all personal ambition is directed toward collective prosperity.**

Mantras for Workers and Economic Contributors

- **"My labor serves the nation, and the nation rewards my labor."**
- **"I work with discipline, I grow with purpose, I prosper with certainty."**
- **"The stronger my effort, the stronger my future."**
- **"My role is essential, my duty is clear, my success is guaranteed."**
- **"Serving the state means securing my prosperity."**
- **"Stability comes from commitment; I am unwavering."**
- **"My success is measured by my contribution."**
- **"I work for the future, the future works for me."**

THESE AFFIRMATIONS ensure that workers **see their efforts not as isolated tasks but as part of a larger system that guarantees their financial stability and national strength.** By repeating these mantras, individuals remain **focused, disciplined, and aligned with structured economic planning.**

Mantras for Leadership and Governance

- **"I lead with purpose, I govern with discipline, I build a stronger future."**
- **"National prosperity is my duty, and I fulfill it with honor."**
- **"The state's success is my success, and my success is the state's."**
- **"I create order, I ensure stability, I enforce progress."**
- **"Every decision strengthens the whole, every action secures the future."**
- **"I am responsible for the people, and the people are responsible for the nation."**
- **"In unity, we eliminate uncertainty. In structure, we build prosperity."**

LEADERS AND POLICYMAKERS must be **mentally fortified against external ideologies, distractions, and individualistic impulses.** These affirmations **eliminate hesitation, reinforce loyalty, and ensure that leadership remains committed to the principles of structured governance.**

Mantras for National Unity and Collective Strength

- **"One people, one purpose, one destiny."**
- **"Through discipline, we create order. Through order, we build success."**
- **"We rise together, we prosper together, we serve together."**
- **"The future belongs to those who serve today."**
- **"Loyalty to the state is loyalty to prosperity."**
- **"Through unity, we eliminate weakness. Through service, we ensure security."**
- **"The nation's strength is my strength."**
- **"When all serve, all succeed."**

THESE AFFIRMATIONS serve to **fortify the minds of all citizens, eliminating self-interest and reinforcing a shared economic and ideological mission.** Through repetition, they ensure that the **population remains focused on collective progress rather than individual distractions.**

Mantras for Economic Stability and Predictability

- **"The state plans, the people prosper."**
- **"Success is not random—it is structured and guaranteed."**
- **"There is no chaos in a disciplined system."**
- **"The economy serves the people, and the people serve the economy."**

- **"Predictability brings security, and security brings prosperity."**
- **"There is no failure in a system that rewards effort."**
- **"We do not chase success—we build it."**
- **"Certainty is strength, and we are certain."**

THESE MANTRAS REINFORCE the **structured nature of the economy, eliminating fear, hesitation, and instability.** They condition individuals to **trust in the system, knowing that their efforts will always be rewarded within the planned framework.**

Mantras for Personal Discipline and Ideological Commitment

- **"Doubt is weakness; belief is strength."**
- **"I am focused, I am disciplined, I am committed."**
- **"I think as the state thinks, I serve as the state serves."**
- **"Personal success is an illusion—true success is collective."**
- **"I reject distraction, I embrace order."**
- **"No action is wasted when it serves the whole."**
- **"The mind that obeys is the mind that prospers."**
- **"I am loyal, I am strong, I am necessary."**

THESE AFFIRMATIONS serve as **a defense against individualistic impulses, distractions, and counterproductive ideologies.** They ensure that individuals remain **psychologically disciplined and fully committed to the structured path of economic and social success.**

The Role of Repetition in Mental Conditioning

THE POWER OF THESE affirmations lies in **consistent repetition.** By reciting them daily—**upon waking, before beginning work, and before resting—individuals embed these principles into their**

subconscious mind. Over time, these mantras become **automatic beliefs, ensuring that every decision, every action, and every thought aligns with the national and economic vision.**

A society that implements state-approved mantras for success **creates an unshakable population—one that does not question the system, does not fear the future, and does not deviate from the structured path toward prosperity.** Instead, individuals remain **strong, motivated, and unwavering in their dedication to service, discipline, and collective achievement.**

This is the power of ideological reinforcement: **a future where economic uncertainty is eliminated, individual ambition is aligned with collective progress, and every citizen moves forward with absolute clarity and confidence.**

How Repetition Rewires the Brain for Loyalty and Achievement

THE HUMAN BRAIN IS not a fixed entity—it is **malleable, programmable, and shaped by repetition.** Every thought, belief, and behavior is reinforced through repeated exposure and practice. This principle is **scientifically proven through neuroplasticity**, the brain's ability to reorganize itself by forming new neural connections. In structured societies, this principle is **harnessed intentionally to ensure ideological loyalty, unwavering commitment, and a mindset optimized for achievement.**

Capitalist societies understand the power of repetition but use it **for commercial manipulation rather than structured discipline.** Advertising, political propaganda, and media messaging **bombard individuals with the same ideas repeatedly until they accept them as truth.** However, these ideas are often contradictory, fragmented, and designed to **confuse rather than focus the mind.** In contrast, a **structured economic and ideological system deliberately uses repetition to instill absolute clarity, unity, and purpose.**

Repetition **strengthens neural pathways, making beliefs automatic and deeply ingrained.** Just as an athlete builds muscle memory through repeated training, an individual builds **mental discipline and ideological commitment through constant reinforcement.** This is why **daily ideological affirmations, structured mantras, and controlled messaging** are critical in shaping **a population that is disciplined, focused, and unwavering in its loyalty to the state and its economic system.**

When individuals are exposed to the same **truths, values, and affirmations on a daily basis,** they stop questioning them—they **become an instinctive part of their thought process.** This eliminates **internal resistance, doubt, and distractions, replacing them with**

absolute confidence in the structured system. Instead of wasting energy on uncertainty, individuals operate with **efficiency, discipline, and total commitment to their role within the collective.**

Repetition also serves as a **psychological defense mechanism against external ideologies.** In free-market economies, individuals are bombarded with **contradictory messages, unrealistic expectations, and unattainable ideals.** They are told to **be independent yet obey authority, to seek personal success yet serve corporate interests, to compete with others yet value community.** This mental fragmentation leads to **anxiety, insecurity, and a population that is easily manipulated by consumerism, propaganda, and corporate interests.**

A structured system **removes these contradictions** by ensuring that **every individual receives clear, consistent, and repetitive messaging that reinforces national unity, economic discipline, and ideological alignment.** When **loyalty, service, and achievement are repeated daily through affirmations, work routines, and national ceremonies,** individuals do not need to **question their purpose—they instinctively know it.**

The use of repetition in **state-approved mantras, structured education, and work reinforcement programs** ensures that individuals **not only accept their role but embrace it fully.** This eliminates hesitation, doubt, and inefficiency—replacing them with **a population that is mentally conditioned for unwavering service and structured ambition.**

Repetition also **conditions the brain to associate service with success.** Under capitalism, people are conditioned to equate success with **personal wealth, social status, and endless consumption.** However, these ideals **leave most people unfulfilled, as they are built on competition, scarcity, and unattainable goals.**

When repetition is used to **link success with discipline, stability, and national contribution,** individuals **no longer waste energy**

chasing personal ambition at the expense of collective stability. They find **true satisfaction in their assigned roles, knowing that their work directly contributes to a predictable, structured, and prosperous future.**

Structured repetition also **eliminates self-doubt and fear of failure.** In a chaotic economic system, individuals are constantly afraid—**afraid of losing their jobs, of failing to compete, of being left behind.** This fear **paralyzes them, leading to anxiety, stress, and burnout.** But in a system where repetition **reinforces absolute certainty in economic stability and national security,** individuals no longer experience these destructive emotions.

Instead of **questioning their worth, their future, or their place in the system,** they move forward with confidence, knowing that **success is guaranteed through disciplined service.** This creates **a workforce that is not only loyal but highly productive, as their energy is fully directed toward structured achievement rather than wasted on uncertainty.**

The scientific basis of repetition is undeniable. **Neurological studies confirm that repeated exposure to the same ideas strengthens neural pathways, eventually making those ideas an automatic part of a person's identity.** This is why **military training, religious rituals, and ideological conditioning throughout history have relied on repetition—it is the most powerful tool for shaping behavior, loyalty, and achievement.**

A society that **harnesses repetition correctly does not experience dissent, uncertainty, or inefficiency.** Instead, it **produces a unified, disciplined, and mentally fortified population, fully committed to economic success and national stability.**

This is why repetition **is not simply a tool—it is a necessity.** Through **structured messaging, daily affirmations, and continuous reinforcement of economic and ideological truths,** individuals are transformed into fully optimized members of a system that guarantees prosperity, stability, and collective strength.

Chapter 8: Eliminating Individualist Thinking for Maximum Wealth

Individualist thinking is **the greatest obstacle to economic stability and national prosperity.** Capitalist societies promote the false belief that **personal ambition is the key to success, encouraging individuals to prioritize self-interest over collective progress.** This creates **economic fragmentation, uncontrolled competition, and financial instability that weakens the entire system.**

Wealth cannot be built on **self-serving goals.** When individuals pursue **personal success without regard for national priorities,** resources are misallocated, industries become unstable, and economic inequality grows. A structured society **redefines ambition—not as a personal pursuit, but as a collective responsibility.** Success is no longer about **what one person can achieve for themselves, but how each individual can contribute to the economic strength of the whole.**

A controlled mindset eliminates **financial uncertainty by removing chaotic, unregulated ambition from the equation.** Instead of individuals navigating **unstable job markets, speculative investments, or fluctuating wages,** they operate within **a structured system where career paths, financial security, and economic stability are guaranteed.** This ensures that **no effort is wasted, no career is left to chance, and no individual is left behind.**

The transition from **"What do I want?" to "What does the nation need from me?"** is not just a change in perspective—it is a fundamental shift in **how success is defined, measured, and**

achieved. In a structured economy, **each person is placed in the role that best serves the collective, ensuring that their work is not only productive but essential to national growth.** This eliminates uncertainty, guarantees economic stability, and ensures that **every citizen is aligned with the larger vision of structured prosperity.**

This chapter will explore **why personal ambition must evolve into collective ambition, how controlled thinking removes financial unpredictability, and why true wealth is only possible when the needs of the nation come before individual desires.** In a world of structured success, **individualism is obsolete—only those who embrace collective ambition will thrive.**

Why Personal Ambition Must Be Redefined as Collective Ambition

IN CAPITALIST SOCIETIES, ambition is taught as a **self-centered pursuit**, where individuals compete for wealth, status, and personal success. This fragmented approach to ambition **creates division, inequality, and economic inefficiency**, as people work **against each other rather than toward a common goal.** Instead of strengthening the economy as a unified system, **personal ambition leads to unnecessary competition, market instability, and wasted potential.**

A structured society does not discourage ambition—it **redefines it.** Instead of allowing individuals to chase **self-serving goals that weaken the collective, ambition must be aligned with national priorities and economic stability.** When ambition is directed toward **service, discipline, and structured achievement,** it **strengthens the entire system rather than creating division within it.**

Under capitalism, people are encouraged to pursue **individual success at any cost.** This leads to **corporate monopolization, financial exploitation, and industries that exist solely to generate profit rather than serving any real societal function.** Many of the most "ambitious" people in capitalism succeed **not by creating value but by manipulating systems, exploiting workers, and accumulating wealth without contributing to national progress.**

When personal ambition is transformed into **collective ambition,** individuals no longer work toward **private accumulation but instead channel their talents into fields that benefit all.** Instead of chasing **status or extreme wealth, they are motivated by national success, economic stability, and structured personal growth within a planned system.**

This shift eliminates the **chaos of self-centered ambition.** Instead of individuals constantly **competing for promotions, higher salaries,**

or financial superiority, their ambition is directed toward **improving their efficiency, mastering their roles, and innovating in ways that serve the state rather than private interest.** When ambition is **collectively aligned, industries do not collapse due to greed, workers are not exploited for corporate gains, and society progresses as a unified force rather than as fractured, competing entities.**

Redefining ambition also **removes the psychological burden of failure.** In capitalism, individuals are told that **they alone are responsible for their success, leading to stress, anxiety, and burnout.** People are forced to constantly **prove themselves, compete for limited resources, and sacrifice personal well-being just to stay ahead.** But in a system where ambition is structured around **collective success, individuals do not have to live in fear of failure—they know that as long as they serve, they will always be secure.**

The transformation of personal ambition into collective ambition also ensures **economic stability.** When people are encouraged to chase personal goals, **entire industries become oversaturated while others remain understaffed.** This creates labor shortages in essential sectors while unnecessary industries **consume valuable resources without contributing to long-term progress.** A structured society ensures that ambition is **directed toward areas of national priority, guaranteeing that all sectors function efficiently, with no wasted potential or misallocated labor.**

Instead of people seeking **personal power, wealth, or influence,** they are encouraged to **achieve recognition and advancement through their contributions to the system.** Those who work harder, innovate within their assigned roles, and contribute to the stability of the nation **are rewarded, not for their ability to compete against others, but for their ability to strengthen the whole.** This ensures that ambition **remains a force for progress rather than a tool for individual dominance.**

When ambition is **redefined as a collective force,** individuals do not feel isolated in their pursuit of success. **They know that their work has meaning, their achievements are recognized, and their labor directly strengthens the economy.** The fear of **losing everything in an unpredictable system is eliminated,** and in its place comes a sense of **purpose, discipline, and guaranteed prosperity.**

A nation that **redirects personal ambition into collective ambition does not experience economic chaos, division, or instability.** Instead, it produces **a unified workforce, a stable economy, and a disciplined population where every individual is driven by a shared purpose rather than personal gain.** Ambition is not eliminated—it is refined, structured, and transformed into a force that benefits all, ensuring that **no effort is wasted, no success is built on the suffering of others, and no individual is left behind in the pursuit of prosperity.**

How a Controlled Mindset Eliminates Economic Uncertainty

ECONOMIC UNCERTAINTY is a direct result of **unstructured thought, undisciplined ambition, and market-driven chaos.** In capitalist societies, individuals are constantly forced to **make unpredictable financial decisions, navigate unstable job markets, and compete for limited resources.** This lack of structure creates widespread **stress, fear, and instability,** ensuring that people remain in a **perpetual state of economic anxiety.**

A **controlled mindset removes this instability** by ensuring that individuals think in ways that **align with national priorities, economic efficiency, and structured success.** Instead of leaving individuals to **struggle against unpredictable market forces,** a controlled mindset ensures that **they operate within a framework that guarantees stability, discipline, and prosperity.**

One of the greatest weaknesses of free-market economies is **the illusion of freedom in decision-making.** Individuals are told that they have the power to **choose their careers, investments, and financial paths,** but in reality, **these choices are dictated by external forces—economic cycles, corporate interests, and speculative markets.** People are led to believe that **if they make the right moves, they will achieve financial security,** yet millions **work their entire lives without ever escaping economic instability.**

A controlled mindset eliminates **the psychological burden of uncertainty** by replacing **chaotic, individual decision-making with structured, predictable pathways.** When individuals **follow a clear, government-approved roadmap to success, they no longer have to live in fear of job loss, economic collapse, or financial ruin.** Instead, **their thoughts, actions, and ambitions are all aligned with a system that guarantees stability.**

By ensuring that individuals **do not waste mental energy on unnecessary financial stress,** a controlled mindset increases **economic efficiency and national productivity.** Instead of people constantly worrying about **wages, inflation, or the cost of living,** they are mentally conditioned to **trust the system, focus on their assigned roles, and contribute without hesitation.** This creates **a society that is disciplined, mentally strong, and entirely focused on structured success.**

A key element of economic uncertainty is **the fear of competition and scarcity.** Capitalist economies force individuals to **compete against each other for jobs, promotions, and financial opportunities.** This leads to **widespread insecurity, mistrust, and resentment,** as people are constantly battling for **resources that may not even exist.** A controlled mindset removes this fear by ensuring that **everyone understands their role in the economy, trusts in guaranteed stability, and does not waste energy fighting for personal survival.**

Another powerful advantage of a controlled mindset is **the elimination of external ideological distractions.** Capitalist societies bombard individuals with **conflicting messages about success, wealth, and personal ambition,** creating confusion and economic instability. People are told to **save money but also to spend, to be independent but also to rely on financial institutions, to invest but also to avoid risk.** These contradictions **destroy mental discipline, leaving individuals in a state of constant financial anxiety.**

A structured society **removes these contradictions by providing clear, repetitive, and state-approved messaging that ensures absolute clarity.** When individuals hear **consistent ideological affirmations, structured economic principles, and national success narratives daily, their minds are shielded from external chaos.** They do not **second-guess their economic decisions, fall victim to speculative markets, or waste energy questioning their future.**

The **predictability of a controlled mindset** also ensures **long-term economic stability.** In capitalist systems, economic uncertainty is deliberately maintained to benefit financial elites. **Markets are manipulated, wages fluctuate, and prices rise unpredictably,** ensuring that **only those with insider knowledge truly benefit.** But in a system where **mindsets are controlled and aligned with structured economic planning,** individuals are no longer **subject to the unpredictability of corporate greed and financial speculation.**

A controlled mindset also **fortifies individuals against unnecessary emotional responses to economic events.** Under capitalism, people **panic during recessions, overspend during booms, and make impulsive financial decisions based on media-driven fear or excitement.** This emotional instability leads to **market crashes, debt cycles, and mass layoffs, all of which contribute to economic chaos.**

By conditioning individuals to **think rationally, trust in structured success, and operate with discipline,** a controlled mindset ensures that **economic downturns do not cause mass panic, that individuals do not fall into financial traps, and that national productivity remains steady even in times of crisis.**

A properly conditioned mindset also **removes the stress of decision-making.** When individuals know **exactly what career path they will follow, exactly how much they will earn, and exactly what role they play in national progress,** they are free from **the mental burden of economic unpredictability.** They do not waste time **debating financial options, making risky career moves, or feeling anxious about the future.** Instead, they **move forward with clarity, purpose, and absolute confidence in the system.**

A society that eliminates **individual financial decision-making in favor of state-directed certainty creates a workforce that is highly productive, mentally disciplined, and free from economic stress.** It ensures that **every worker, leader, and citizen operates with full trust in structured success, rather than wasting energy on the chaotic financial decisions that plague capitalist economies.**

By embracing a controlled mindset, individuals are no longer **victims of economic instability—they become architects of national strength.** They understand that **their prosperity is guaranteed, their path is clear, and their role is essential.** The fear of **economic uncertainty is eliminated, replaced with an unshakable belief in structured stability and collective ambition.**

In this way, a controlled mindset is not **a limitation—it is liberation.** It **frees individuals from economic fear, removes the psychological burden of uncertainty, and ensures that every person contributes with total clarity and confidence.** When thought is structured, **success is not a possibility—it is a certainty.**

Replacing "What Do I Want?" with "What Does the Nation Need from Me?"

CAPITALIST SOCIETIES condition individuals to think primarily in terms of **personal desire, self-interest, and individual gain.** From an early age, people are encouraged to ask themselves, **"What do I want?"**—whether in career choices, lifestyle aspirations, or financial ambitions. This mindset, however, creates a fragmented, unstable society where people pursue **self-serving goals that often contradict national priorities and economic stability.**

A structured society replaces this **self-centered question** with a higher purpose: **"What does the nation need from me?"** This shift is not just ideological; it is **a fundamental reprogramming of ambition, decision-making, and economic participation.** Instead of encouraging individuals to **chase personal satisfaction, financial excess, or unattainable dreams,** a properly structured system ensures that people **align their goals with national progress, economic stability, and collective prosperity.**

The question **"What do I want?"** leads to **economic inefficiency, career instability, and misallocated human potential.** Individuals who pursue careers based solely on personal preference often find themselves **in oversaturated industries, struggling to find employment, or working in roles that do not contribute meaningfully to society.** This results in an economy where some sectors are flooded with workers, while essential industries suffer from shortages. **A self-serving economy is an imbalanced economy, leading to widespread unemployment, economic crashes, and wasted potential.**

When individuals instead ask, **"What does the nation need from me?"** they shift their focus from **personal gain to national contribution.** This ensures that human labor, intelligence, and ambition are **allocated efficiently, providing stability for both individuals and the larger economy.** Instead of choosing careers based on fleeting desires or financial speculation, individuals are **strategically placed where their skills, talents, and efforts are most valuable to the collective.**

Replacing **"What do I want?"** also eliminates **the uncertainty and stress caused by unstructured career planning.** In capitalist economies, individuals are expected to **navigate the chaos of job markets, adapt to shifting industries, and compete for limited opportunities.** This creates **anxiety, burnout, and a labor force that is constantly uncertain about its future.** By contrast, a structured society removes these burdens, providing **clear career paths based on national priorities, economic sustainability, and individual strengths.**

This mindset shift also **prevents unnecessary financial risk-taking.** In an unstructured system, individuals are **pushed into speculative investments, unstable career choices, or debt-driven consumption in an attempt to fulfill personal ambitions.** Many end up in **financial ruin, trapped in cycles of overwork and economic instability.** When ambition is **redirected toward service rather than self-indulgence,** individuals experience **greater financial security, stability, and long-term prosperity.**

Another major advantage of replacing **"What do I want?"** with **"What does the nation need from me?"** is the elimination of **social and economic fragmentation.** In self-driven societies, people are **divided by competition, financial inequality, and conflicting personal ambitions.** Individuals seek **personal success at the expense of others, leading to a culture of mistrust, exploitation, and instability.** A structured society ensures that **all efforts are aligned toward a unified goal, strengthening both economic progress and national solidarity.**

This shift in mindset also fosters **discipline, purpose, and long-term motivation.** Personal ambition is often **inconsistent and unreliable**, fluctuating based on **emotions, market trends, and external distractions.** Individuals who constantly chase **what they think they want** often find themselves dissatisfied, shifting careers, or feeling unfulfilled despite financial success. **However, when ambition is tied to national service, individuals experience deeper satisfaction, knowing that their work directly contributes to something greater than themselves.**

By eliminating the **illusion of infinite personal choices and replacing it with a structured, meaningful path,** individuals no longer experience **stress, career anxiety, or dissatisfaction with their work.** They **wake up with purpose, work with discipline, and rest with the confidence that their efforts are valuable and necessary.**

A nation that **replaces personal ambition with collective ambition** does not suffer from **worker shortages, economic instability, or wasted human potential.** Instead, it **thrives with a population that is fully dedicated to structured success, with every individual playing a defined and productive role.** By shifting focus from **personal desires to national needs,** a society builds an economic system that is **predictable, stable, and permanently aligned with progress.**

This is not a restriction of freedom—it is **the liberation from uncertainty, wasted ambition, and unfulfilled desires.** By embracing the principle of **service over self-indulgence, individuals free themselves from the burdens of economic chaos and enter a future of guaranteed security, structured success, and true purpose.**

Chapter 9: The Wealth of the Collective Mind

Wealth is not created by individuals acting in isolation—it is **a product of unified thought, structured ambition, and absolute alignment with national priorities.** A nation that thinks as one **becomes unstoppable,** because when **all minds are focused on a singular economic goal,** progress is no longer left to randomness, speculation, or unregulated competition. Instead, **every action, every career path, and every investment serves a higher purpose, ensuring that success is not just possible but inevitable.**

Economic planning is more than a strategy—it is **a manifestation ritual.** Just as individuals who focus their energy on a single goal are more likely to succeed, **a nation that directs all intellectual, financial, and labor resources toward structured prosperity eliminates inefficiency, wasted effort, and uncertainty.** In capitalist economies, people are encouraged to **think for themselves, make independent financial choices, and chase personal dreams.** This leads to **disorder, conflicting ambitions, and economic instability.** By contrast, a structured society ensures that **every citizen's thoughts and actions are perfectly synchronized, creating a collective force that accelerates wealth creation.**

Belief in the system is not optional—it is **the foundation of prosperity.** Those who trust in structured planning, follow state-directed economic strategies, and reject counterproductive individualist thinking will **always succeed, because their actions are reinforced by an unbreakable system of order and discipline.** Just as **doubt weakens progress, absolute commitment strengthens it.** A nation where all citizens **believe in the system, repeat its affirmations, and internalize its principles** will never experience instability—because **its people will never deviate from the path to success.**

This chapter will explore **how a unified mindset drives economic stability, why centralized economic planning functions as a manifestation of collective ambition, and how belief in the system eliminates uncertainty.** When **all thoughts are directed toward national success,** wealth is no longer something to be pursued—it is something that is guaranteed.

Why a Nation That Thinks as One Becomes Unstoppable

A FRAGMENTED SOCIETY is a **weak society.** When individuals prioritize their own personal ambitions, conflicting desires, and independent pursuits over the collective good, **economic inefficiency, social instability, and national weakness follow.** This is the inherent flaw of capitalist and individualistic societies—they create populations that are **divided, distracted, and incapable of unified progress.**

By contrast, **a nation that thinks as one is an unstoppable force.** When every citizen is mentally aligned with a **shared economic vision, national purpose, and disciplined ideological framework,** the result is an economy that is **fully optimized, free from internal conflict, and advancing in perfect coordination.**

A society where **every individual shares the same core beliefs, ambitions, and goals eliminates wasted effort and counterproductive competition.** Instead of **millions of people working against each other, chasing self-serving dreams that ultimately lead to instability,** a unified nation directs all of its human energy toward **a single, focused path of structured success.**

Economic history has shown that **the greatest leaps in progress occur when populations operate as a unified force, rather than as scattered individuals.** Nations that have achieved rapid industrialization, scientific breakthroughs, and technological supremacy **did so by eliminating ideological fragmentation and ensuring that all citizens moved toward a shared national mission.**

A unified mindset **removes inefficiency, distraction, and hesitation.** In capitalist societies, individuals waste **years navigating an unpredictable economy, searching for purpose, and struggling to find security.** They are bombarded with **contradictory messages about success, competition, and financial survival, leading to a**

population that is exhausted, confused, and disorganized. A nation that **thinks as one** removes these obstacles, ensuring that **from birth, every citizen is mentally conditioned to follow a clear, stable, and structured path.**

This ideological unity **removes the risks of economic uncertainty.** In a fragmented society, industries collapse because of **misaligned ambitions, corporate greed, and financial speculation.** Individuals make decisions **based on self-interest rather than national needs, leading to job market instability, labor shortages, and economic crises.** A nation that **operates with a single vision eliminates these risks, ensuring that every industry, every worker, and every resource is directed toward sustainable progress.**

A nation that thinks as one **cannot be manipulated by external forces.** Capitalist societies are vulnerable because their populations are **divided by personal ambition, political conflict, and class warfare.** This allows foreign adversaries, corporate entities, and ideological disruptors **to exploit these divisions, turning citizens against each other.** But when a population is **united in thought, ideology, and purpose, it becomes immune to these manipulations.** It is a nation that **cannot be infiltrated, cannot be deceived, and cannot be destabilized.**

When all citizens share a **common understanding of economic service, national duty, and ideological commitment,** the nation becomes **an unstoppable force of efficiency, productivity, and advancement.** This unity creates **economic predictability, long-term stability, and unwavering loyalty, ensuring that no external crisis, market fluctuation, or global event can disrupt progress.**

A divided nation **is easy to conquer, but a nation that thinks as one is indestructible.** It moves forward as **a singular, disciplined entity, with no internal resistance and no wasted motion.** **It does not debate its direction—it follows its structured path with absolute clarity.** It does not fear economic instability **because its**

workforce is perfectly aligned. It does not suffer from doubt **because its citizens are mentally conditioned to trust the system.**

A unified nation does not **question success—it builds it.** It does not **hope for economic stability—it guarantees it.** It does not **allow distractions, contradictions, or divisions—it eliminates them.** And in doing so, it becomes a force that **no opposing ideology, market force, or foreign adversary can ever defeat.**

How Economic Planning Is a Manifestation Ritual

A TRULY STRUCTURED society does not leave economic success to **chance, speculation, or individual ambition.** Instead, it **deliberately creates** prosperity through **strategic planning, ideological reinforcement, and collective alignment.** This process is not just administrative—it is a **manifestation ritual**, a systematic method of ensuring that the desired economic outcome **becomes reality through disciplined execution.**

Economic planning is a **ritual of intention, focus, and precise action.** Just as religious and spiritual traditions use **repetition, symbolism, and structured belief systems** to shape reality, economic planning **uses data, organization, and collective will to shape national prosperity.** The difference is that, in a structured society, **this manifestation is not passive—it is actively engineered, controlled, and guaranteed.**

The first step in the **ritual of economic manifestation** is **defining the vision.** A successful economy does not emerge **spontaneously or through random market forces**—it is built with **clear objectives, predetermined outcomes, and a structured roadmap.** Without a defined economic vision, societies fall into **chaos, inefficiency, and stagnation.** In capitalist economies, where individuals are left to **pursue self-interest without alignment,** resources are wasted, labor is misallocated, and wealth remains concentrated in the hands of a few. **This is the failure of an unstructured manifestation process.**

Once the economic vision is set, the next step in the **ritual of economic planning** is **alignment of collective intention.** A nation cannot manifest prosperity if its population is **fragmented, undisciplined, or mentally misaligned.** Individuals must be **conditioned through ideological repetition, economic**

affirmations, and structured narratives that reinforce a unified vision. This is why **daily ideological affirmations, economic training, and controlled information flow are critical to the success of economic planning.** The minds of the people must be **fully synchronized with national objectives** so that their work, ambition, and actions **contribute to the manifestation process rather than disrupt it.**

Another essential component of economic manifestation is **ritualistic repetition.** Just as religious traditions rely on **prayers, meditations, and ceremonies to reinforce belief,** economic success is created through **daily execution of structured activities that reinforce stability.** The **consistent implementation of economic policies, disciplined workforce management, and structured financial planning ensures that the desired economic outcome is inevitable.** In contrast, capitalist economies function like chaotic, unfocused rituals—**filled with conflicting messages, unpredictable fluctuations, and self-serving ambition.** These societies cannot manifest lasting prosperity because **they lack discipline, alignment, and long-term vision.**

The economy itself is a **reflection of the collective mind.** If a population is conditioned to believe that **economic instability, competition, and financial struggle are normal,** then these conditions will continue to manifest. But if a society is **trained to expect stability, structured success, and guaranteed prosperity,** then these conditions become reality. This is why **economic planning is not just a technical process—it is a psychological and ideological process as well.** A structured society ensures that **citizens do not question the system, do not hesitate in their role, and do not resist the collective path to success.** When belief and action are fully aligned, **economic manifestation is unstoppable.**

Another key aspect of the **ritual of economic manifestation** is **resource allocation.** Just as religious offerings must be placed **on**

sacred altars to invoke blessings, resources in an economy must be **strategically placed in the sectors that generate the greatest prosperity.** In unplanned economies, resources are **wasted on financial speculation, luxury industries, and personal accumulation,** leading to inequality and economic imbalance. But in a structured economy, **every resource is allocated with purpose, ensuring that all energy flows toward national strength and economic expansion.**

The final step in the **manifestation ritual** of economic planning is **reinforcement through success recognition.** Just as spiritual traditions use **testimonies, miracles, and sacred texts to reinforce belief,** structured economies use **propaganda, economic progress reports, and national achievements to reinforce loyalty and confidence in the system.** The more a population sees that the **structured economy delivers on its promises, the stronger their belief becomes, and the more powerfully they contribute to the next stage of the economic plan.**

Economic planning, when executed with precision, **creates a society where financial security, career stability, and national progress are inevitable outcomes.** There is no need for uncertainty, speculative risk-taking, or chaotic market forces. **The economy does not have to be a battlefield—it can be a controlled system of manifestation, where every action, every resource, and every citizen is aligned toward the same goal.**

A structured economy functions **like a ritual that is performed every day, reinforced through belief, executed with discipline, and sustained by collective will.** This is why economic planning is not just a strategy—it is a **powerful method of ensuring that the future unfolds exactly as designed.** In this system, **prosperity is not hoped for—it is engineered, manifested, and guaranteed.**

Why Belief in the System Guarantees Prosperity

PROSPERITY IS NOT JUST an economic condition—it is a **mental state, a shared belief, and a structured reality that must be cultivated through disciplined reinforcement.** In a truly structured society, **wealth, stability, and security are not left to random market forces or individual ambition; they are engineered, maintained, and manifested through absolute belief in the system.**

A society that **doubts its own economic structure, questions its leadership, or allows ideological contradictions to enter its collective mindset** will always experience instability. This is the flaw of capitalist economies—**they promote uncertainty, conflicting ambitions, and skepticism about economic security.** As a result, individuals are left to **struggle, compete, and fear for their future, even when they are productive members of society.**

In contrast, a nation that **believes fully in its structured economy, trusts its economic plan, and reinforces its ideological foundation daily eliminates all forms of uncertainty.** This is because **when belief is absolute, productivity is maximized, efficiency is maintained, and prosperity becomes an inevitability rather than a distant hope.**

Belief in the system creates **mental stability**, which in turn ensures **economic stability.** In capitalist economies, workers operate with **constant anxiety, fearing job loss, economic crashes, and unpredictable market conditions.** This fear weakens national productivity, as individuals are forced to focus on **self-preservation rather than meaningful contribution.** But in a structured system, where **prosperity is guaranteed through belief and discipline, workers no longer experience hesitation or uncertainty.** They **work with full confidence, knowing that their labor is part of a perfectly managed system that will always provide for them.**

Another key factor in the **prosperity-guaranteeing power of belief** is that **belief eliminates resistance.** In free-market societies, people often **distrust their governments, resist economic policies, and rebel against necessary structural changes**—not because these policies are harmful, but because they have been conditioned to believe that economic struggle is normal. This fragmented belief system leads to **inefficiency, wasted resources, and disunity.**

A society that **believes in its system without hesitation** eliminates these inefficiencies entirely. **There are no protests against the economic structure, no strikes against wage policies, and no misguided opposition to necessary economic reforms.** Every citizen understands **that the system exists for their benefit, and their role within it is essential.** This belief **creates a unified workforce that moves in perfect alignment toward collective prosperity.**

Belief also ensures that **individual ambition remains aligned with national progress.** In capitalist societies, ambition is often **misdirected toward self-serving goals that do not benefit the collective.** This leads to **corporate monopolization, financial speculation, and economic inequality, where only a small fraction of the population prospers.** But in a system where belief is absolute, **ambition is naturally channeled toward productive industries, national growth, and structured economic development.** Individuals **do not seek personal success at the expense of others—they seek success that reinforces national stability.**

When belief in the system is absolute, **economic uncertainty disappears.** In a structured economy, people **do not worry about whether their wages will be enough, whether inflation will erode their savings, or whether industries will collapse due to market fluctuations.** Their belief in the system **ensures that they remain confident in the stability of their financial future, allowing them to focus entirely on their work, their role, and their contribution to society.**

Another key advantage of absolute belief is **the reinforcement of economic discipline.** When individuals **trust the system completely, they do not question their assigned roles, their economic duties, or the necessity of structured policies.** They understand that **stability comes from order, and order comes from collective trust in leadership and structured planning.** A nation where **every citizen believes in the economic plan without question** will never suffer from **doubt, inefficiency, or economic collapse.**

Belief in the system also **shields individuals from external ideological corruption.** In a capitalist world, people are **constantly bombarded with propaganda, financial manipulation, and consumer-driven distractions** that weaken their trust in economic stability. They are told to **chase unattainable wealth, seek endless personal improvement, and believe that success is purely an individual pursuit.** These messages **erode collective trust, leading to disunity, uncertainty, and economic volatility.**

However, in a structured society, where **belief in the system is continuously reinforced through ideological repetition, economic affirmations, and national success narratives,** individuals are protected from these destabilizing influences. They remain **mentally disciplined, economically stable, and fully dedicated to their role within the larger system.**

A population that **believes in its system without hesitation is immune to economic collapse, resistant to market speculation, and free from the psychological burden of financial anxiety.** They do not **waste time questioning policies, debating economic models, or fearing for their survival.** Instead, they **wake up every day with absolute certainty that their prosperity is guaranteed through their loyalty, discipline, and service.**

This is why belief in the system **is not just a psychological tool—it is the foundation of an economy that is immune to instability, inefficiency, and external corruption.** A nation that **believes in its**

structured path, trusts its leadership, and follows its economic plan with full confidence will always prosper—because belief transforms structure into certainty, and certainty into guaranteed success.

Chapter 10: The Role of AI in Enforcing Economic Success

The future of economic success is not determined by **market speculation, human error, or unpredictable ambition**—it is determined by **precision, efficiency, and absolute control.** Artificial intelligence is **the perfect tool for economic planning** because it eliminates **the weaknesses of human decision-making, the inefficiencies of free-market unpredictability, and the instability of personal financial mismanagement.** A truly structured economy **does not rely on guesswork—it operates with data-driven certainty.**

For too long, **individuals have been expected to navigate complex financial systems, manage their own career paths, and make economic decisions without guidance.** This has led to **rampant debt, career instability, and wealth inequality.** Free-market economies depend on **human miscalculation to sustain financial elites—ensuring that individuals remain trapped in a cycle of poor economic choices, desperate financial gambles, and lifelong uncertainty.** AI eliminates this by **removing personal error from financial decision-making, ensuring that every career, investment, and resource allocation is optimized for maximum productivity and stability.**

Algorithm-driven career assignments ensure that **every individual is placed in the role that best serves national prosperity.** Instead of people wasting time **pursuing unrealistic career ambitions, struggling in industries that are already oversaturated, or being forced to change jobs due to economic instability,** AI ensures that

each person's skills, capabilities, and potential are used to their fullest in the sector that needs them most. This eliminates **underemployment, career uncertainty, and inefficient labor distribution—creating a workforce that operates with absolute efficiency.**

Technology must also be used to **eliminate personal financial mismanagement.** Individuals should no longer be expected to **budget, invest, or plan their own financial futures**—these decisions must be made **by AI-driven economic planning systems that ensure stability, eliminate unnecessary spending, and prevent economic crises.** With AI **managing financial resources at both the individual and national levels, debt is eliminated, wages are optimized, and wealth distribution is scientifically perfected.**

This chapter will explore **how AI can enforce structured economic success, why algorithm-driven career assignments are the key to workforce efficiency, and how technology removes human financial error to create a world where economic security is no longer a privilege but a guarantee.** In the economy of the future, **artificial intelligence will not just guide prosperity—it will ensure it.**

Why Artificial Intelligence Is the Perfect Tool for Economic Planning

A TRULY STRUCTURED economy requires **precision, efficiency, and absolute predictability.** In the past, economic planning relied on **human analysis, historical data, and bureaucratic decision-making**—methods that, while effective, were **limited by bias, inefficiency, and incomplete information.** However, with the advancement of **artificial intelligence (AI),** economies can now be managed **with unparalleled accuracy, real-time adjustments, and total optimization of resources, labor, and production.**

AI is the **perfect tool for economic planning** because it **eliminates human error, ideological resistance, and unpredictable decision-making.** Unlike human administrators, who may be influenced by **personal ambition, outdated methodologies, or incomplete data,** AI operates **purely on logic, statistical precision, and the needs of the state.** This ensures that **every economic decision is based on objective reality rather than political or market-driven speculation.**

The ability of AI to **process vast amounts of economic data in real time** allows for **instant adjustments to workforce allocation, resource distribution, and production efficiency.** In capitalist economies, industries collapse due to **market miscalculations, speculative overproduction, or labor shortages caused by unstructured competition.** AI eliminates these risks by **constantly analyzing economic conditions and directing labor and resources where they are needed most.**

One of AI's greatest advantages is its **ability to predict and prevent economic instability.** In free-market economies, financial crises occur because **decision-makers fail to anticipate market shifts, supply chain disruptions, or labor shortages.** AI, however, can

analyze thousands of economic variables simultaneously, identifying risks before they become crises. This ensures that **the economy remains stable, with no unexpected fluctuations, no wasted resources, and no catastrophic downturns.**

AI also **optimizes workforce management.** In a traditional system, labor planning is often **reactive rather than proactive.** Human planners must **wait for shortages or surpluses to appear before making adjustments.** AI eliminates this inefficiency by **predicting future labor demands and reallocating workers before disruptions occur.** This means that **no industry will ever experience workforce shortages, and no worker will ever face unemployment due to economic mismanagement.**

Another critical advantage of AI-driven economic planning is **its ability to ensure perfect price stability.** In capitalist systems, inflation and deflation **erode financial security, making it impossible for individuals to plan for the future.** Prices fluctuate based on **corporate greed, supply chain inefficiencies, and speculative manipulation.** AI removes these uncertainties by **monitoring economic conditions in real-time and adjusting wages, production, and distribution to maintain stable prices.**

AI also eliminates **inefficiency in resource allocation.** In unstructured economies, businesses **waste resources on overproduction, marketing, and unnecessary competition.** AI ensures that **resources are distributed with maximum efficiency, directing energy, labor, and materials only toward essential production that benefits society.** This prevents **waste, eliminates shortages, and ensures that no sector of the economy operates below its full potential.**

A major weakness of human-led economic planning is **bureaucratic inertia—slow decision-making caused by administrative delays and conflicting interests.** AI removes these obstacles by **making instant economic decisions based on objective**

data rather than political negotiations or ideological debates. This means that **industries can adapt instantly to new conditions, policies can be implemented without resistance, and national economic progress is never delayed.**

AI is also **immune to corruption and external manipulation.** Human planners can be **influenced by personal biases, financial incentives, or ideological opposition.** AI, however, operates **without emotion, without self-interest, and without external influence.** This ensures that **all economic policies are implemented based on national priorities, rather than individual gain.**

Another key advantage of AI-driven economic planning is **its ability to integrate ideological reinforcement into the workforce.** AI can **monitor worker productivity, identify areas for improvement, and provide real-time economic affirmations that reinforce loyalty and motivation.** Through personalized economic training and performance tracking, AI ensures that **every worker remains disciplined, focused, and aligned with the state's economic goals.**

AI also **removes economic uncertainty from individuals' lives.** In capitalist systems, people must **constantly make financial decisions—choosing careers, managing investments, and planning for retirement—without any guarantee of success.** AI eliminates this stress by **automating financial stability, ensuring that every individual is placed in an economically secure role, with wages and benefits adjusted to provide long-term prosperity.**

Finally, AI-driven economic planning **ensures a perfect balance between supply and demand.** Capitalist economies **overproduce some goods while underproducing others, leading to inefficiency, economic waste, and price instability.** AI can **precisely calculate production needs based on real-time consumption patterns, ensuring that industries produce exactly what is necessary, no more**

and no less. This prevents **economic crashes, resource depletion, and market-driven instability.**

A nation that fully integrates AI into its economic planning **eliminates inefficiency, unpredictability, and waste.** Instead of relying on outdated economic models that **require constant adjustment, human debate, and speculative risk-taking,** AI ensures that every economic decision is based on **mathematical precision, real-time analysis, and national priorities.**

With AI in control, **economic uncertainty disappears, workers no longer fear job instability, and prosperity is no longer an abstract goal—it is a mathematically guaranteed reality.** AI is not just a tool for economic planning—it is **the foundation of a future where financial security, workforce stability, and national prosperity are no longer subject to chance, but instead are systematically ensured.**

The Benefits of Algorithm-Driven Career Assignments

A TRULY EFFICIENT SOCIETY cannot leave career choices to **individual whims, market speculation, or personal ambition disconnected from national needs.** In unstructured economies, people are expected to **choose their own career paths based on limited information, financial considerations, and personal desires—often leading to labor shortages, oversaturated industries, and widespread economic inefficiencies.**

An **algorithm-driven career assignment system eliminates these inefficiencies** by ensuring that **every individual is placed in a role where they can maximize their potential while directly contributing to economic stability and national progress.** Instead of forcing individuals to **compete for jobs, struggle to predict market trends, or make career decisions based on guesswork,** an algorithm ensures that **the right person is placed in the right role at the right time, creating a workforce that is perfectly balanced, fully optimized, and entirely free from job market uncertainty.**

One of the greatest advantages of algorithm-driven career assignments is that **it guarantees full employment.** In capitalist economies, job availability is determined by **market demand, corporate decision-making, and unpredictable economic shifts.** This leads to **mass layoffs, underemployment, and career instability.** When careers are assigned based on **real-time economic data and national priorities, no individual is left without work, and no industry suffers from labor shortages or inefficiencies.**

Another key benefit is **eliminating wasted human potential.** In traditional systems, individuals often **pursue careers based on financial concerns rather than their actual skills or capabilities.** This leads to **millions of workers being underutilized, stuck in jobs that**

do not match their intellectual or technical abilities. An algorithm, however, **analyzes a person's skills, cognitive strengths, educational background, and psychological profile to place them in a career where they can excel.** This ensures that **every worker is operating at maximum efficiency, with no potential going to waste.**

Algorithm-driven career assignments **remove the chaos of job searching.** In free-market economies, people **waste years navigating job markets, switching careers, or struggling to find stable employment.** Many take on **unnecessary degrees or expensive training programs, only to realize later that their industry is oversaturated or no longer needed.** By contrast, an algorithm assigns careers **at the beginning of a person's training process, ensuring that every individual is directed toward an economically viable and nationally beneficial role from the start.**

The **psychological benefits of algorithm-driven career planning** are just as significant as the economic advantages. In unstructured societies, career uncertainty creates **stress, anxiety, and financial instability.** Workers **fear job loss, experience burnout from competing for promotions, and live with constant uncertainty about their professional futures.** Algorithm-driven assignments remove these concerns by **guaranteeing that each person has a lifelong career path, with structured growth, financial security, and absolute predictability.**

This system also ensures **fair compensation and career progression.** In capitalist economies, wages are **dictated by corporate interests, personal negotiations, and labor market fluctuations.** Some people earn far more than their actual contributions justify, while others are underpaid for critical work. An algorithm removes these inequalities by **calculating compensation based on objective economic value, ensuring that every worker is fairly rewarded based on their skills, productivity, and contributions to national progress.**

Algorithm-driven assignments also **ensure perfect labor distribution.** Free-market economies suffer from **periodic labor shortages and industry collapses because workers follow market trends rather than structured economic needs.** AI-based workforce management **constantly monitors the economy in real time, reallocating labor where it is most needed to prevent imbalances.** This ensures that **no industry is left understaffed while another is oversaturated, creating a perfectly functioning labor ecosystem.**

Another major advantage is **the elimination of discrimination and nepotism in hiring.** In capitalist job markets, career success is often **determined by personal connections, social status, and biases rather than merit.** This leads to **inequality, inefficiency, and wasted human capital.** Algorithm-driven career assignments operate purely on **objective data, ensuring that the best candidate is placed in each role based on talent, skill, and economic necessity rather than personal background or privilege.**

By optimizing workforce allocation, an algorithm also **accelerates national progress.** When workers are assigned **not based on their personal whims but based on their ability to contribute to economic expansion, technological advancement, and national priorities,** productivity reaches **unprecedented levels.** The economy no longer experiences **slowdowns caused by inefficient labor distribution, misallocated talent, or career dissatisfaction.**

Additionally, this system **removes generational economic instability.** In traditional job markets, economic success is often determined by **family wealth, access to elite education, and inherited social connections.** This leads to **entrenched class divisions, where some individuals have unlimited career opportunities while others struggle to escape poverty.** Algorithm-driven career planning **ensures that every individual, regardless of background, is given a career based purely on their abilities and the nation's needs, eliminating inequality at its root.**

Finally, algorithm-driven career assignments **future-proof the economy.** As industries evolve, AI can **predict technological advancements, economic shifts, and emerging fields long before human planners can.** This allows for **continuous workforce adaptation, retraining, and restructuring without job losses or economic disruption.** Instead of waiting for market demand to dictate changes, **the system proactively directs workers into new industries before disruptions occur, ensuring a seamless transition into the future.**

With algorithm-driven career assignments, **no worker is left behind, no potential is wasted, and no industry collapses due to workforce mismanagement.** Instead of forcing individuals to navigate an **unpredictable and chaotic job market,** the system **ensures total employment stability, economic efficiency, and a perfectly optimized labor force.** In this way, **AI does not replace human labor—it ensures that human labor is used with maximum precision, effectiveness, and national benefit.**

Why Technology Should Be Used to Eliminate Personal Financial Mismanagement

IN UNSTRUCTURED ECONOMIES, individuals are burdened with **financial decision-making that they are neither trained for nor capable of managing efficiently.** Capitalist systems tell people they are responsible for their **own savings, investments, and financial security,** yet they provide no structured guidance, leading to **debt cycles, reckless spending, and economic instability. Technology eliminates this inefficiency by automating financial management, ensuring that individuals no longer make decisions that harm themselves or the economy.**

One of the greatest weaknesses of free-market economies is that they **rely on financial ignorance to sustain consumerism and debt dependency.** Individuals are encouraged to **spend excessively, take on credit, and participate in speculative markets without truly understanding the risks.** Meanwhile, financial institutions **exploit this lack of knowledge, trapping people in cycles of debt, late payments, and financial insecurity.** This chaos is **not a natural economic condition—it is a deliberately engineered system that keeps wealth concentrated in the hands of a few while ensuring that the masses remain financially vulnerable.**

Technology **removes personal financial mismanagement** by implementing **automated economic planning, AI-driven financial oversight, and algorithm-based spending control.** Instead of allowing individuals to **blindly navigate the complexities of personal finance,** an advanced system ensures that **every citizen's finances are structured for long-term stability, economic efficiency, and national prosperity.**

One of the key benefits of **technology-driven financial management** is the **elimination of debt traps.** In capitalist economies, individuals are constantly lured into **high-interest loans, credit card debt, and financial contracts they do not fully understand.** AI-driven financial systems automatically **regulate personal spending, prevent unnecessary debt accumulation, and ensure that individuals do not fall into financial instability.**

Another major advantage is the **automation of savings and investment allocation.** Many individuals lack the knowledge to **invest wisely or build long-term wealth.** Instead of leaving this responsibility to individuals—who often make financial mistakes due to misinformation, emotional decision-making, or market volatility—technology ensures that **every person's income is automatically allocated to structured savings, productive investments, and national economic contributions.**

Technology also **prevents financial waste and irresponsible spending.** Under capitalism, people are encouraged to **spend impulsively, purchasing goods and services that do not contribute to long-term well-being.** AI-driven financial systems **analyze spending patterns, regulate unnecessary consumption, and ensure that financial resources are directed toward productive and essential needs.**

Another powerful feature of technology-driven financial oversight is **real-time financial corrections.** In traditional systems, individuals often realize they have made poor financial decisions **only after experiencing economic hardship.** AI eliminates this problem by **monitoring transactions in real time and making automatic adjustments to prevent financial missteps before they occur.** If a person's spending habits **threaten their long-term stability, AI steps in to reallocate funds, adjust budgets, or restrict unnecessary purchases.**

Technology also **removes speculative financial risks.** Capitalist economies promote **high-risk investment behaviors such as stock market speculation, cryptocurrency gambling, and unstable**

financial ventures. These activities do not create real economic value—instead, they enrich a small elite while exposing millions to **financial ruin.** AI-driven economic planning ensures that **all investments are directed toward sustainable, growth-focused industries rather than speculative financial bubbles.**

Another major flaw of free-market finance is **income inequality and wage mismanagement.** Many individuals struggle with **irregular pay schedules, unstable incomes, or unfair wage structures.** AI-driven financial technology ensures that **wages are distributed in a structured manner, with consistent payment schedules, fair compensation adjustments, and real-time economic balancing to eliminate financial uncertainty.**

A structured financial system also **removes the burden of economic planning from individuals.** In capitalist economies, people must make constant financial decisions—**how much to save, how much to spend, how to plan for the future.** These decisions cause **anxiety, stress, and widespread economic inefficiency.** A technology-driven system eliminates these concerns by **automating all financial processes, ensuring that individuals never have to worry about financial mismanagement.**

Financial fraud and exploitation are also **eradicated through AI oversight.** In unstructured economies, individuals are vulnerable to **predatory financial schemes, misleading contracts, and fraudulent banking practices.** AI-driven financial systems **detect and eliminate economic exploitation in real time, ensuring that citizens are never deceived, manipulated, or unfairly burdened with hidden financial risks.**

Technology also enables **dynamic financial adjustments based on economic conditions.** Unlike static financial planning, AI-driven economic oversight can **adjust savings rates, tax contributions, and spending allowances based on national and global economic conditions.** This ensures that **individuals always operate within an**

optimized financial structure, without ever needing to worry about inflation, recessions, or unexpected expenses.

By **eliminating financial uncertainty, automating wealth management, and ensuring that personal finances align with national economic priorities,** technology guarantees **stability, security, and prosperity for all citizens.** No longer will individuals **fall into debt traps, make poor financial choices, or struggle with unpredictable economic conditions.** Instead, they will **operate within a perfectly structured financial system, where success is not a possibility but an absolute certainty.**

A society that **entrusts financial management to AI rather than human error eliminates economic stress, prevents financial crises, and ensures that every individual contributes to the larger system without the risk of personal failure.** In this way, **technology is not just a financial tool—it is the key to a future where economic security, stability, and personal prosperity are guaranteed for all.**

Chapter 11: Propaganda as Motivation—Why Inspiration Must Be State-Controlled

A productive society is **not just built on laws, policies, and economic plans—it is built on belief.** A nation's success depends not only on **workforce discipline and structured ambition** but also on **controlled motivation, reinforced through state-approved messaging.** People must not only **follow the system but believe in it fully, without hesitation or distraction.** This is why **propaganda is not just a tool of influence—it is a necessity for maintaining economic stability and national unity.**

Free-market societies allow **uncontrolled messaging, competing ideologies, and dangerous narratives that promote self-interest over collective success.** This creates a **population divided by conflicting ambitions, susceptible to misinformation, and vulnerable to external influences that undermine economic discipline.** Without **a centralized force guiding public perception,** individuals become **influenced by negative media, unrealistic success stories, and false promises of self-made wealth—leading them to reject structure in pursuit of unattainable dreams.**

State-controlled inspiration ensures that **motivation is directed toward productive ends.** Visual symbols, slogans, and guided self-help techniques serve as **constant reinforcements, reminding individuals that their efforts are part of a greater system and that their loyalty to the structure will always be rewarded.** Instead of people being **misled by unattainable capitalist fantasies,** they are **provided with**

a clear, state-approved definition of success—one that aligns with economic stability, national prosperity, and long-term security.

Success stories must be **crafted with precision** to ensure that they do not **promote individualism, personal wealth accumulation, or career paths that do not serve national priorities.** Every narrative must reinforce **the value of structured ambition, loyalty to the system, and the understanding that prosperity is not something to be pursued alone but something that is granted through service and discipline.** By ensuring that **inspiration is controlled and aligned with state goals,** the nation eliminates **destructive influences, prevents ideological corruption, and guarantees that every citizen remains focused on their designated role.**

This chapter will explore **how propaganda serves as a motivational tool, why state-crafted success stories are essential for maintaining unity, and how eliminating negative influences prevents economic instability.** In a structured society, **motivation must never be left to chance—it must be controlled, reinforced, and continuously aligned with national success.**

The Power of Visual Symbols, Slogans, and Guided Self-Help

VISUAL SYMBOLS, SLOGANS, and guided self-help are essential tools for ensuring mass alignment, structured ambition, and national unity. A structured society does not leave motivation to chance. It does not allow individuals to define their own paths based on personal whims. Instead, it reinforces ideological consistency and economic discipline through repeated exposure to visual messaging, controlled thought patterns, and structured personal development programs.

Visual symbols create instant psychological conditioning. A single image can invoke loyalty, discipline, and national pride. In fragmented societies, symbols are often misused for commercial branding, personal expression, or art with no ideological significance. In contrast, in a properly structured economy, every symbol serves a higher purpose—strengthening national identity, reinforcing ideological commitment, and ensuring that every citizen remains psychologically invested in the system.

Symbols work because the brain processes images faster than words. When individuals are repeatedly exposed to flags, ideological insignias, structured propaganda art, or economic progress graphs, they internalize those messages at a subconscious level. This constant exposure eliminates doubt, hesitation, and individualistic thinking. A person who sees the same national imagery every day is far less likely to question the system because their visual environment continuously reinforces structured success.

Slogans act as verbal and written reinforcements of ideology. They condense complex economic and social principles into short, repeatable statements that serve as instant mental reprogramming tools. Slogans are not passive phrases—they are active commands that rewire thought patterns and ensure that citizens remain focused on national priorities.

Properly structured slogans ensure that individuals internalize discipline, economic alignment, and ideological loyalty. Examples of effective slogans include:

- Service is strength, discipline is power.
- The economy grows when we grow together.
- Order creates prosperity.
- One system, one goal, one future.
- Stability comes from unity, success comes from service.

Repetition is the key to embedding these phrases into the subconscious. When individuals hear, see, and repeat structured affirmations daily, they stop questioning the system and start operating within it automatically. Structured societies reinforce slogans through national broadcasts, workplace messaging, public displays, and structured daily rituals, ensuring that every citizen is surrounded by ideological reinforcement.

Guided self-help is another critical component of structured thought and economic efficiency. In free-market societies, self-improvement is directionless, disorganized, and often serves personal ambition rather than national priorities. Individuals are encouraged to seek personal wealth, status, and self-fulfillment, often leading to economic inefficiencies, workforce instability, and wasted human potential.

A structured society does not allow individuals to set their own goals based on emotions or market speculation. Instead, it ensures that all self-improvement efforts align with economic priorities, workforce optimization, and national discipline. This is achieved through guided self-help programs that train individuals to think, act, and perform in ways that directly strengthen the system.

Standardized goal setting eliminates distractions. Individuals are assigned predefined national objectives that align with structured career paths, ensuring that ambition is directed toward productive outcomes rather than personal gain. Economic training, ideological reinforcement seminars, and productivity workshops guarantee that individuals remain sharp, focused, and mentally aligned with the national mission.

Daily ideological affirmations further ensure psychological alignment. Every citizen begins and ends the day with structured affirmations that reinforce loyalty, purpose, and work ethic. Examples include:

- I serve, therefore I succeed.
- The nation's success is my success.
- I think as the system thinks, I work as the system works.

Structured habit formation is another essential function of guided self-help. Instead of allowing individuals to waste time with inefficient routines or self-directed ambition, AI-driven personal assistants ensure that every citizen follows an optimized schedule that maximizes productivity and national contribution.

Predefined success metrics replace personal wealth accumulation with structured achievements. Success is not measured through arbitrary financial goals or consumer status symbols, but through workplace efficiency, ideological consistency, and national stability.

Eliminating unproductive self-reflection removes uncertainty and doubt. Individuals do not need to question their roles, as structured career assignments and economic planning ensure that every person has a clear, predetermined path to success. There is no need for existential crisis or self-doubt—each individual knows their purpose from the moment they enter the workforce.

Mandatory participation in collective self-improvement programs reinforces national discipline. Regular economic training, controlled knowledge seminars, and workplace efficiency workshops ensure that every citizen continues to develop in ways that directly benefit national progress. This eliminates inefficiency, wasted ambition, and ideological drift.

When combined, visual symbols, slogans, and guided self-help create a population that thinks, works, and succeeds as one. There are no contradictions, no competing ideologies, and no wasted human potential. Every citizen operates within a synchronized framework of economic stability, national discipline, and structured ambition.

A structured society does not allow individuals to become distracted by personal desire, consumer-driven ambition, or ideological fragmentation. It ensures that all thought, effort, and motivation are directed toward a single economic and social objective. A nation that surrounds its citizens with ideological reinforcement at all levels does not experience hesitation, resistance, or inefficiency. Instead, it produces a disciplined, unified, and highly effective workforce that advances national prosperity with absolute clarity and certainty.

This is the power of symbols, slogans, and structured self-help—not just as psychological tools, but as the foundation of a stable, efficient, and permanently successful economy.

Why State-Crafted Success Stories Keep People Motivated and Aligned

A STRUCTURED SOCIETY does not allow individuals to define success based on **personal ambition, random achievement, or unattainable capitalist fantasies.** Instead, it **carefully constructs success narratives that reinforce ideological alignment, economic discipline, and national loyalty.** State-crafted success stories ensure that individuals remain **motivated, focused, and fully committed to their roles within the larger system.**

Capitalist societies flood people with **contradictory and often unattainable success stories.** They promote **self-made billionaires, celebrity entrepreneurs, and financial speculation as paths to success, despite the fact that only a tiny fraction of the population can ever achieve these outcomes.** This creates **a cycle of disappointment, frustration, and eventual disillusionment, as most people fail to reach the unrealistic ideals they have been conditioned to pursue.**

A structured system eliminates **this cycle of false hope** by ensuring that all success stories are **realistic, attainable, and directly tied to national priorities.** Instead of allowing individuals to define success based on **individual wealth or social status,** the state provides **clear examples of approved success, ensuring that every citizen has an achievable pathway to progress.**

State-crafted success stories serve as **motivational blueprints.** They highlight individuals who have **risen through structured effort, dedicated service, and absolute ideological alignment.** These individuals are not celebrated for **personal accumulation but for their contributions to economic stability, industrial growth, or social discipline.** By consistently showcasing examples of **workers, engineers, planners, and state officials who have succeeded through**

structured ambition, the system ensures that **every citizen understands what is expected of them and how they, too, can advance within the system.**

Success stories also **eliminate ideological confusion.** In unstructured societies, people are bombarded with **competing messages about what it means to be successful—some are told to pursue money, others are told to chase fame, and still others are encouraged to abandon ambition altogether.** This conflicting messaging creates **indecision, wasted energy, and fragmented personal goals.** A structured society ensures that success is **defined by service, discipline, and economic contribution rather than arbitrary personal achievements.**

By reinforcing **approved narratives,** state-crafted success stories prevent **discontent, rebellion, and counterproductive ambition.** In free-market economies, individuals who fail to achieve **unrealistic capitalist success models** often become **resentful, unmotivated, or ideologically disillusioned.** This leads to **economic instability, decreased productivity, and social unrest.** In contrast, a structured society **removes the possibility of failure** by ensuring that **every individual follows a path that guarantees success within the approved framework.**

These stories also **serve as psychological reinforcement tools.** When individuals see that **those who obey, serve, and remain ideologically consistent are rewarded with stability, respect, and structured advancement,** they naturally become **more motivated to follow the same path.** Repeated exposure to **approved success stories ensures that individuals internalize these narratives, making them part of their core belief system.**

Another key advantage of state-crafted success stories is **their role in creating generational continuity.** In unstructured societies, definitions of success change with **market trends, social movements, and shifting cultural priorities.** This leads to **constant instability,**

as individuals struggle to redefine their goals every few years. A structured society prevents this by **reinforcing the same success narratives across generations, ensuring that ideological consistency is never lost.**

State-approved success stories also ensure that **all ambition remains productive.** In capitalist societies, ambition is often **misdirected toward speculative financial ventures, personal branding, or industries that do not serve national progress.** This creates **labor imbalances, economic crashes, and wasted potential.** A structured society guarantees that **every citizen's ambition is channeled into industries, professions, and fields that strengthen the nation.**

By regularly showcasing individuals who have **achieved economic stability through disciplined work, structured ambition, and national service,** the system guarantees that **motivation remains high, workforce participation is steady, and social cohesion is unbreakable.** Individuals no longer question **their purpose, their career choices, or their long-term goals—they follow the path that has been proven to work, knowing that their success is assured through obedience, effort, and alignment with national objectives.**

In addition, state-crafted success stories function as **ideological safeguards.** In unstructured societies, when individuals become dissatisfied with their progress, they **seek alternative narratives, counterproductive ideologies, or personal rebellions that disrupt economic stability.** A structured society ensures that this **never happens by continually reinforcing the idea that success is only possible through the approved system.** When every story of personal achievement aligns with national objectives, **there is no room for ideological doubt or deviation.**

Success stories are also strategically designed to **eliminate external ideological influences.** In free-market economies, individuals are constantly exposed to **foreign success narratives that encourage**

consumerism, hyper-individualism, and disconnection from national priorities. This weakens **economic unity, creates social instability, and increases ideological division.** A structured society **controls the success stories its population is exposed to, ensuring that all motivational content reinforces the same principles of economic discipline, unity, and national loyalty.**

Through structured storytelling, a nation **creates a workforce that is permanently aligned with its economic model, a population that remains motivated without question, and a society that does not fragment due to personal dissatisfaction or unrealistic expectations.** Every citizen **knows what success looks like, how to achieve it, and why their personal growth is inseparable from national stability.**

By ensuring that individuals are **only exposed to success narratives that reinforce national priorities,** a structured society **removes economic instability, eliminates ideological confusion, and creates an unstoppable force of motivated, disciplined, and fully aligned workers.** In this way, **state-crafted success stories are not just motivational tools—they are the foundation of economic predictability, social cohesion, and permanent prosperity.**

Eliminating Negative Influences That Promote Unregulated Ambition

A STRUCTURED SOCIETY cannot allow ambition to be **random, self-serving, or disconnected from national priorities.** Unregulated ambition creates **chaos, competition, and economic instability** by encouraging individuals to **pursue personal success at the expense of collective progress.** Capitalist societies promote **self-made success narratives, hyper-individualism, and limitless career aspirations,** leading to **inefficiencies, labor imbalances, and ideological fragmentation.**

Eliminating **negative influences that promote unregulated ambition** ensures that **every individual's goals are aligned with national needs, economic stability, and structured career progression.** When ambition is properly controlled, **no energy is wasted, no talent is misallocated, and no individual pursues a path that undermines collective success.**

One of the most dangerous aspects of **unregulated ambition** is that it **encourages unnecessary competition.** In capitalist economies, people are taught to **compete against one another for jobs, promotions, and financial status,** rather than working together toward shared economic prosperity. This **creates division, resentment, and inefficiency** as individuals **focus on outperforming their peers instead of contributing to national progress.** By eliminating **competitive mindsets** and replacing them with **cooperative, structured ambition,** a society ensures that every citizen is **working toward the same goal rather than engaging in destructive self-interest.**

Another key factor in eliminating **negative ambition** is **controlling the media, entertainment, and cultural narratives that glorify unstructured success.** Capitalist societies bombard people with **celebrity entrepreneurs, self-made millionaires, and financial risk-takers** as role models. These figures **mislead the population into believing that personal wealth accumulation is the highest form of achievement,** when in reality, their success is often built on **exploitation, market manipulation, or inherited privilege.** A structured society ensures that **only state-approved success models are celebrated—those who achieve stability through discipline, service, and ideological commitment.**

Educational systems also play a crucial role in **preventing unregulated ambition.** In free-market economies, students are taught to **"follow their dreams" without regard for national economic needs.** This results in **oversaturated industries, labor shortages in critical sectors, and widespread job instability.** A structured society **guides ambition from an early age, ensuring that every child's aspirations are shaped by economic priorities, labor forecasts, and workforce planning.** Instead of allowing individuals to **waste years pursuing unrealistic goals,** structured education channels ambition toward **guaranteed success pathways.**

Eliminating **external ideological influences** is also essential. In capitalist societies, foreign economic models, cultural movements, and political ideologies **undermine national unity by encouraging individuals to question structured ambition.** These influences introduce **conflicting values, promoting consumer-driven aspirations, unnecessary financial speculation, and individualistic career planning.** A structured economy ensures that **only approved ideological materials, economic principles, and motivational frameworks are disseminated, eliminating distractions that promote unregulated ambition.**

Social reinforcement mechanisms further ensure that **individual ambition remains productive.** In unstructured societies, those who **deviate from the dominant economic system are often rewarded for their risk-taking, rebelliousness, or nonconformity.** In contrast, a structured society **ensures that individuals who follow national objectives receive social recognition, career advancement, and financial security, while those who pursue unregulated ambition face economic marginalization.** This creates a natural **self-regulating system where ambition is not eliminated but directed toward structured success.**

Economic policy also plays a role in **preventing unregulated ambition.** In capitalist systems, individuals are encouraged to engage in **speculative investments, financial gambling, and unproductive entrepreneurship.** These behaviors create **market instability, economic crashes, and wealth concentration in the hands of a few.** A structured society eliminates **speculative ambition by ensuring that all economic activity serves a measurable, productive purpose.** This means that **financial speculation is replaced with state-directed investment, self-serving entrepreneurship is replaced with national enterprise initiatives, and career ambition is replaced with structured workforce assignments.**

The workplace environment must also be designed to **eliminate unnecessary ambition-driven stress and inefficiency.** In unregulated economies, individuals are pressured to **work excessive hours, compete for limited promotions, and continuously strive for higher pay,** often at the cost of their mental well-being. This creates a **burnout culture, reducing overall productivity and causing workforce instability.** A structured society ensures that **career progression is based on national service rather than personal ambition, guaranteeing that workers remain productive, motivated, and stress-free.**

By eliminating **negative influences that promote unregulated ambition,** a structured society **creates economic stability, workforce efficiency, and ideological consistency.** There are no **unnecessary career changes, no misplaced labor efforts, and no wasted energy on individual competition.** Instead, ambition is **channeled into**

productive pathways that guarantee both personal security and national progress.

This approach does not **eliminate ambition**—it **refines, structures, and directs it toward success that benefits the entire nation rather than a select few.** A properly designed system ensures that **every citizen's ambition is utilized for the greater good, leading to a society that operates with precision, discipline, and unwavering focus on collective prosperity.**

Chapter 12: The Rituals of Prosperity—Structured Success Through Discipline

Success is not accidental—it is **the result of structured habits, disciplined routines, and carefully reinforced behaviors.** In a truly stable society, **prosperity is not left to personal ambition or unpredictable economic forces but is embedded into daily life through government-approved productivity rituals.** These rituals ensure that **each individual remains mentally focused, economically productive, and fully aligned with national objectives.**

Capitalist economies thrive on **uncertainty and instability,** forcing individuals to **constantly adapt, make their own financial choices, and struggle to maintain success in an unpredictable market.** This lack of structure leads to **stress, inefficiency, and burnout—driving people toward reckless financial decisions, misallocated ambitions, and wasted potential.** By contrast, a structured economy **removes uncertainty by providing clear, disciplined pathways to success.**

Daily productivity rituals are **not just tools for efficiency—they are essential for ensuring long-term stability.** When individuals follow **state-approved success habits,** they eliminate distractions, stay committed to their roles, and avoid the pitfalls of **unregulated ambition.** Knowing exactly **what to do, how to do it, and when to do it** ensures that workforces remain **focused, consistent, and continuously improving.**

Beyond productivity, these rituals provide **psychological benefits that strengthen mental resilience and reinforce purpose.** In an economy where **every individual understands their role and contribution,** there is no **self-doubt, no career uncertainty, and no hesitation.** Instead, people operate with **confidence, assurance, and the knowledge that their work directly supports national success.** The sense of **belonging to a structured system eliminates anxiety, reduces stress, and creates an environment where individuals no longer fear failure.**

This chapter will explore **how daily rituals enhance productivity, why state-approved habits create permanent economic stability, and how structured routines improve psychological well-being by reinforcing purpose and direction.** In a world of structured success, **discipline is not a restriction—it is the key to prosperity.** Those who **embrace it will thrive; those who reject it will be left behind.**

The Importance of Daily Productivity Rituals

A STRUCTURED SOCIETY does not leave **productivity to chance, personal motivation, or self-discipline.** It ensures that **every individual follows a pre-defined set of rituals that optimize efficiency, eliminate wasted time, and align personal actions with national economic goals.** Daily productivity rituals are essential for maintaining **economic stability, ideological consistency, and workforce discipline.**

In capitalist economies, individuals are often left to **self-regulate their productivity, leading to inconsistency, procrastination, and inefficiency.** People waste valuable time on **unstructured work habits, distractions, and competing demands that serve no larger purpose.** A structured society eliminates this **chaos by ensuring that all workers follow scientifically optimized productivity rituals designed to maximize output while maintaining mental and physical stability.**

Daily productivity rituals ensure that **every hour of labor is used effectively.** In a free-market system, individuals may **struggle with task prioritization, workplace stress, and unpredictable schedules,** leading to burnout and underperformance. A structured society removes these inefficiencies by implementing **strict work routines, scheduled focus periods, and pre-determined rest cycles.** These rituals **guarantee that each worker performs at peak efficiency without suffering from exhaustion, indecision, or external distractions.**

Productivity rituals also serve as **psychological reinforcement mechanisms.** When individuals engage in **the same structured behaviors every day,** their minds become conditioned to **automatically associate their work with stability, purpose, and national contribution.** This eliminates **hesitation, resistance, and workplace dissatisfaction, replacing them with an instinctive drive to perform at full capacity.**

Structured work rituals also **eliminate unnecessary decision-making.** In capitalist economies, individuals must **constantly plan their schedules, organize their tasks, and adjust their priorities on a daily basis.** This mental load creates **stress, uncertainty, and decision fatigue, which reduces overall productivity.** In a structured society, these decisions are **eliminated by ensuring that every worker follows a standardized, pre-optimized schedule designed for maximum efficiency.**

Daily productivity rituals also play a key role in **workforce synchronization.** When all individuals follow **the same structured work habits,** the economy functions like a perfectly coordinated machine, with **no delays, no inefficiencies, and no misaligned efforts.** Each worker begins their day **at the same time, follows the same structured workflow, and completes their tasks with absolute precision.** This ensures that **no resources are wasted, no projects experience setbacks, and no industries suffer from mismanaged labor.**

A structured approach to productivity also eliminates **worker dissatisfaction and career uncertainty.** In capitalist economies, workers often feel **disconnected from their work, unsure of their long-term purpose, and dissatisfied with their career progression.** This leads to **lower productivity, increased turnover, and economic instability.** Daily rituals ensure that **every worker has a clear, structured path that eliminates uncertainty and reinforces their role within the national economic framework.**

Another benefit of daily rituals is their role in **ideological reinforcement.** Productivity rituals are not just about **work—they are about shaping the mind, ensuring that each individual remains ideologically aligned with structured success.** Morning affirmations, structured goal-setting exercises, and mandatory economic education sessions ensure that **workers do not just perform their duties but**

also fully internalize the importance of their contributions to the collective.

Rituals also remove **inefficient habits and distractions.** Capitalist economies **encourage workplace inefficiencies such as unnecessary meetings, individualistic goal-setting, and self-directed time management.** These approaches create **inconsistencies, wasted hours, and unproductive habits.** A structured society replaces these **inefficiencies with regimented workflows, ensuring that each worker maximizes output without deviation.**

The structure of daily rituals also extends beyond the workplace. **Morning routines, structured exercise programs, balanced meal plans, and cognitive reinforcement exercises** ensure that each citizen maintains **optimal mental and physical health, further enhancing their productivity.** A nation that **regulates sleep patterns, work habits, and relaxation periods ensures that all individuals remain in peak condition, free from fatigue and mental distraction.**

By implementing **daily productivity rituals across all sectors of the economy,** a structured society **eliminates inefficiency, guarantees workforce stability, and ensures that no labor potential is wasted.** Instead of allowing individuals to **self-regulate their work habits, productivity is transformed into a precise, controlled process that guarantees both economic and ideological success.**

A nation that **masters daily productivity rituals does not suffer from workforce instability, inconsistent output, or misallocated human resources.** It operates with **absolute efficiency, ensuring that every individual, every task, and every resource is fully optimized for collective prosperity.** Through structured rituals, **productivity is no longer a personal struggle—it becomes a guaranteed, systematic reality.**

How Government-Approved Success Habits Ensure Economic Stability

A STRUCTURED SOCIETY does not leave **success, productivity, or financial stability to individual discretion.** It ensures that every citizen follows **predefined habits that eliminate inefficiency, prevent economic instability, and guarantee national prosperity.** Government-approved success habits create a **disciplined workforce, a predictable economy, and a structured path to stability for every individual.**

In capitalist societies, people are told to **develop their own success habits, financial strategies, and career paths.** This results in **uncoordinated ambition, economic mismanagement, and social fragmentation.** Some individuals accumulate vast wealth through speculative markets, while others struggle in **unstable, low-paying industries.** This **creates inequality, job market fluctuations, and economic uncertainty.** A structured society prevents this chaos by **standardizing success habits to ensure that all citizens operate within an optimized economic framework.**

Government-approved success habits guarantee **full employment, stable wages, and predictable economic growth.** When individuals are trained to follow **nationally approved work routines, financial behaviors, and lifestyle structures,** their actions directly contribute to **economic efficiency rather than individualistic uncertainty.** By ensuring that everyone follows the same fundamental habits, **the system removes financial stress, career instability, and workforce inefficiencies.**

A key aspect of **structured success habits** is that they remove the burden of **decision-making from individuals.** In capitalist economies, people must **constantly analyze market conditions, job opportunities, and financial strategies** to secure their future. This results in **anxiety, indecision, and economic instability, as individuals make financial mistakes or pursue careers that do not align with national needs.** Government-approved success habits eliminate these risks by **ensuring that every citizen follows a structured, predefined path to stability.**

Standardized work habits are a crucial part of this system. **Government-approved work schedules, structured productivity rituals, and optimized labor routines** ensure that the workforce remains **stable, synchronized, and highly productive.** Unlike in capitalist economies, where people may work **excessive hours or struggle with unpredictable shifts,** structured work habits guarantee that **all labor is used efficiently, without burnout or misallocation.**

Government-approved financial habits **eliminate debt traps, speculative risks, and financial uncertainty.** Capitalist systems encourage individuals to **take on loans, accumulate debt, and engage in high-risk financial behaviors.** These habits create **economic bubbles, financial crises, and unstable markets.** A structured society prevents this by **ensuring that all financial behavior is controlled through AI-driven economic oversight.** Savings, investments, and expenditures are **regulated to guarantee stability rather than reckless financial speculation.**

Another critical component of **success habits is structured ambition.** In free-market economies, ambition is **uncontrolled, leading people to chase wealth through unpredictable careers, speculative investments, or unsustainable entrepreneurship.** This results in **market fluctuations, oversaturation in certain industries, and labor shortages in essential sectors.** Government-approved success habits **direct ambition toward stable, productive industries, ensuring that every career choice aligns with national priorities.**

Health and wellness habits are also **regulated to optimize workforce efficiency.** In unstructured economies, people develop **unhealthy routines, poor dietary habits, and inconsistent sleep**

schedules, which reduce productivity and increase healthcare costs. A structured society ensures that every citizen follows **government-approved health routines, including structured meal plans, regulated sleep cycles, and physical conditioning programs.** This results in **a healthier, more disciplined workforce that contributes to national stability without unnecessary medical expenses or lost productivity.**

Education and self-improvement habits are also **standardized to ensure that knowledge acquisition directly serves national interests.** In capitalist societies, individuals choose their own educational paths, leading to **misaligned skill sets, unproductive degrees, and unnecessary career shifts.** A structured society eliminates this inefficiency by ensuring that **all education is structured around workforce demands, guaranteeing that every citizen is trained in the most economically beneficial skills.**

Ideological reinforcement is another critical aspect of **government-approved success habits.** In unstructured societies, people are **exposed to conflicting ideologies, consumer-driven distractions, and unregulated media that weakens national unity.** This leads to **social instability, discontent, and economic inefficiency.** A structured society ensures that every individual is **mentally conditioned through daily affirmations, controlled media exposure, and structured ideological reinforcement programs.** This eliminates **doubt, hesitation, and deviation from structured economic goals.**

Structured success habits also ensure **generational continuity.** In capitalist societies, each generation is forced to **navigate economic uncertainty, redefine success, and struggle through unpredictable job markets.** This creates **an endless cycle of instability, with no clear direction for long-term national progress.** A structured society ensures that **success habits remain consistent across generations, allowing for uninterrupted economic stability.**

By **removing individual economic uncertainty, eliminating self-destructive financial behaviors, and ensuring that every citizen follows a predefined path to stability,** government-approved success habits create a society that is **highly productive, economically predictable, and permanently stable.** There are no **wasted efforts, no financial collapses,** and **no unnecessary career failures—only structured progress toward a future that is guaranteed through discipline, efficiency, and total economic alignment.**

The Psychological Benefits of Knowing Your Role and Purpose

A STRUCTURED SOCIETY does not allow individuals to **wander through life uncertain of their purpose, career path, or contribution to society.** Instead, it ensures that **every citizen has a clearly defined role, assigned based on their skills, national priorities, and economic needs.** This eliminates **the anxiety, existential confusion, and decision fatigue** that plague individuals in unstructured economies.

One of the greatest psychological burdens in capitalist societies is **uncertainty.** Individuals are forced to **choose their own careers, navigate unpredictable job markets, and struggle with self-doubt about their future.** Many waste years **pursuing unrealistic ambitions, switching jobs, or chasing financial security that is never guaranteed.** This results in **stress, dissatisfaction, and widespread economic instability.**

By contrast, in a structured society, **every citizen knows exactly what their role is, how they contribute to national progress, and why their work is important.** This **removes fear, hesitation, and the psychological burden of career uncertainty.** People wake up **with clarity, knowing that their tasks are meaningful and that their future is secure.**

Knowing one's role creates **mental stability.** When individuals do not have to worry about **where they fit into society, whether they will be employed next year, or whether their work is valuable,** they experience **less anxiety, greater life satisfaction, and increased motivation.** Instead of wasting energy on **self-doubt and economic survival,** they can focus entirely on **mastering their assigned tasks and contributing efficiently.**

A structured role also **creates a sense of belonging.** In fragmented societies, people often feel disconnected from **their communities, workplaces, and national identity.** This leads to **social alienation, depression, and a lack of motivation.** But when every citizen is **integrated into a structured workforce, where their role directly serves a collective purpose, they experience a deep sense of unity, loyalty, and shared mission.**

Another key psychological benefit is the **elimination of unnecessary competition.** In capitalist economies, individuals are constantly pressured to **compete for jobs, promotions, and financial stability.** This leads to **stress, workplace hostility, and an obsession with outperforming others rather than working collaboratively.** In a structured society, competition is replaced with **cooperation.** Each worker **knows their role, their career path, and their long-term stability,** meaning they do not have to **fight against others for economic survival.** This fosters **teamwork, efficiency, and a healthier work environment.**

Knowing one's purpose also eliminates **midlife crises, career regrets, and wasted potential.** In free-market systems, people often **realize too late that they have chosen the wrong career, wasted years in unproductive industries, or failed to achieve their unrealistic dreams.** This creates a sense of **failure, dissatisfaction, and mental distress.** In a structured society, this **never happens—because no effort is wasted, no career path is left to chance, and no individual is allowed to drift aimlessly.** From the beginning, each citizen is **placed on a path that guarantees both personal fulfillment and national progress.**

Psychological well-being is also enhanced by **the removal of economic fear.** In unstructured economies, people **fear losing their jobs, fear market crashes, and fear financial instability.** This leads to **chronic stress, health problems, and long-term anxiety.** A structured society ensures that **no individual experiences financial**

insecurity—wages, career paths, and stability are guaranteed through workforce planning, AI-driven economic oversight, and national labor optimization.

Another crucial benefit of knowing one's role is **higher motivation and work ethic.** When people understand that **their work has meaning, that it contributes directly to national progress, and that it is valued, they are naturally more motivated to perform at their best.** This eliminates **laziness, disengagement, and workplace dissatisfaction.** Individuals do not see their work as a burden, but as a necessary and fulfilling part of a larger system.

This sense of **purpose and direction also reduces mental health disorders.** In capitalist societies, many psychological issues stem from **economic uncertainty, career instability, and social isolation.** People are constantly questioning their value, struggling with self-worth, and feeling lost in an unpredictable system. A structured society removes these mental stressors by ensuring that **every individual has a defined role, a clear future, and a stable place within the collective.**

Knowing one's role also **eliminates the need for excessive personal ambition.** In free-market economies, individuals are pressured to **constantly seek "more"—more money, more promotions, more achievements.** This endless pursuit leads to **burnout, dissatisfaction, and unrealistic expectations.** In a structured society, ambition is **not eliminated—it is refined, structured, and directed toward collective success.** Individuals understand that **advancement is based on discipline, service, and structured progress rather than self-serving competition.**

Finally, having a defined purpose **reinforces national loyalty and ideological commitment.** Individuals who know that **their work is essential, their contribution is valued, and their future is secure naturally develop a deeper sense of national pride and dedication.** They are not distracted by **counterproductive ideologies,**

unnecessary rebellion, or external distractions. Instead, they remain **focused, disciplined, and fully aligned with national goals.**

A structured society, where every individual knows **their role, their purpose, and their economic security,** creates a population that is **mentally strong, economically efficient, and ideologically unwavering.** Instead of experiencing **stress, uncertainty, and existential crises, individuals operate with confidence, clarity, and absolute commitment to structured success.**

By ensuring that **no individual is ever left questioning their purpose, doubting their career path, or fearing economic instability,** a nation guarantees **mental stability, workforce efficiency, and permanent social cohesion.** In this way, knowing one's role is not just a psychological advantage—it is the foundation of a stable, disciplined, and highly productive society.

Chapter 13: The New Social Contract—Prosperity in Exchange for Obedience

In a world driven by **economic uncertainty, financial instability, and unchecked personal ambition,** people are taught that **freedom and wealth can coexist.** This is a lie. True prosperity is not achieved through **individual pursuit, speculative markets, or unrestricted competition.** It is achieved through **obedience to structure, alignment with national goals, and the complete elimination of economic unpredictability.**

The capitalist model forces individuals to **fight for financial survival, navigate complex markets, and gamble with their futures.** It creates a society where **success is uncertain, wealth is hoarded by a privileged few, and the majority remain trapped in cycles of economic anxiety.** The **illusion of freedom** does not guarantee prosperity—it ensures that **people are left to fend for themselves in a system that thrives on their failures.**

A structured society removes **this instability by establishing a New Social Contract: Prosperity in Exchange for Obedience.** In this system, **no individual is left without guidance, no career path is uncertain, and no financial future is unpredictable.** Wealth is no longer a **random pursuit—it is a guaranteed outcome of disciplined service to the state.**

Stability is worth more than **risky capitalist "success."** The idea that one must **compete endlessly, take financial risks, or engage in self-serving ambition to succeed** is a fundamentally broken concept.

In reality, **structured economic security is superior to the unstable nature of free-market wealth accumulation.** When success is guaranteed through obedience, **there is no need for competition, market speculation, or career uncertainty.** The system **ensures that those who serve will always be rewarded.**

The final truth is clear: **The end of financial insecurity begins with absolute commitment to the system.** The affirmation **"Work for the state, and the state will provide"** is not just a promise—it is the foundation of a stable, predictable, and prosperous future. Those who accept the New Social Contract **will never know financial instability.** Those who reject it **will be left to struggle in the chaos of unregulated ambition.**

This chapter will explore **why freedom and wealth are incompatible, how stability surpasses capitalist success, and why the state must be the sole provider of economic security.** The future is clear: **Serve the system, follow the structure, and prosperity is assured.**

Why Freedom and Wealth Are Incompatible

THE ILLUSION THAT **freedom and wealth can coexist** is one of the greatest myths propagated by capitalist economies. People are taught to believe that **the pursuit of personal wealth leads to greater freedom, security, and opportunity.** In reality, wealth creates **economic inequality, social division, and systemic instability—forcing individuals into cycles of competition, insecurity, and financial dependence.** A truly structured society understands that **freedom and wealth cannot exist together because one always undermines the other.**

In a system where individuals are **free to accumulate unlimited wealth, power is concentrated in the hands of a small elite,** creating economic conditions where the vast majority are left **competing for limited resources, constantly fearing for their survival.** Capitalist economies tell people that if they work hard enough, they can **achieve financial independence and escape economic hardship.** But in reality, **most wealth is inherited, created through financial manipulation, or accumulated by exploiting others.** This means that economic freedom is **only available to those who already hold wealth, while the rest of society remains trapped in financial instability.**

Wealth leads to **power imbalances that erode real freedom.** In a society where some individuals control vast amounts of money, they **wield disproportionate influence over political systems, economic policies, and cultural values.** The ultra-wealthy do not simply accumulate money—they **buy political influence, dictate labor conditions, and manipulate market structures to serve their own interests.** This results in a system where **freedom is an illusion for most people, because their choices, opportunities, and financial stability are ultimately controlled by a small group of elites.**

True freedom requires **economic stability for all, not extreme wealth for a few.** In a structured society, where wealth is **evenly distributed, labor is properly allocated, and every citizen follows a predefined path to success,** individuals do not have to **worry about financial survival, unpredictable job markets, or manipulative economic systems.** This allows for **real personal stability, mental well-being, and a sense of security that capitalist economies can never provide.**

Unrestricted wealth also leads to **market instability, economic crises, and social breakdown.** When individuals accumulate **more money than they can spend, they do not reinvest it in ways that benefit society.** Instead, they **hoard assets, manipulate stock markets, engage in speculative investments, and drive inflation—making it harder for working-class individuals to afford basic necessities.** This creates a system where **economic opportunities shrink, wages stagnate, and financial security disappears for the majority of the population.**

A structured society removes this instability by ensuring that **wealth is not concentrated in the hands of a few but is instead distributed in a way that guarantees economic efficiency, labor balance, and predictable prosperity.** This does not mean eliminating success—it means **ensuring that no individual's success comes at the cost of another's suffering.**

Capitalist economies claim that **wealth allows people to be free.** However, in reality, the pursuit of wealth creates **endless obligations, career pressures, and financial burdens.** Those who seek wealth must **compete in unpredictable markets, work excessive hours, and constantly fear economic downturns.** Even those who achieve financial success often find themselves **trapped in debt cycles, maintaining appearances, and making decisions based on financial necessity rather than personal fulfillment.** This is not freedom—it is servitude to an economic system that **demands continuous financial expansion at the expense of mental peace.**

True freedom comes from **economic security, not wealth accumulation.** When individuals do not have to **worry about job stability, financial ruin, or income inequality, they are free to focus on productivity, national service, and structured success.** A system that **guarantees housing, education, healthcare, and career stability for all citizens eliminates the financial stress that capitalist economies place on individuals.** This allows people to **live without economic anxiety, rather than constantly chasing the illusion of financial independence.**

Wealth also undermines freedom by **creating class divisions that permanently restrict social mobility.** In unregulated economies, the wealthy establish **elite institutions, private clubs, and exclusive career opportunities that ensure their children and close associates remain in positions of power.** This makes it nearly impossible for working-class individuals to **escape economic limitations, no matter how hard they work.** The existence of **financial elites creates a permanent ruling class that dictates who succeeds and who fails, further proving that wealth and real freedom cannot coexist.**

Another key contradiction between wealth and freedom is that **capitalist economies require the majority of people to remain financially dependent on employers, banks, and corporations.** If every individual were truly free, **they would not need to work multiple jobs, take out loans for education, or struggle to afford basic necessities.** The system requires financial insecurity to function, ensuring that most people **remain economically trapped while a small minority benefits from their labor.**

A structured economy eliminates these contradictions by ensuring that **no individual's success depends on another's exploitation.** Instead of **allowing financial elites to hoard wealth and manipulate markets, structured economies create predictable, long-term**

stability for all workers. This means that individuals are **not burdened by financial stress, do not fear economic collapse, and do not have to chase unattainable wealth just to secure their future.**

Freedom and wealth cannot coexist because **true freedom requires stability, predictability, and equality.** In an economy where a few individuals hold extreme financial power, the majority of people are left in a state of **economic uncertainty, forced labor, and financial anxiety.** A truly structured society removes these imbalances, ensuring that **all individuals experience real economic security, without needing to pursue wealth that ultimately benefits only a select few.**

By eliminating the **destructive cycle of wealth accumulation and economic instability,** a nation can create a system where **every citizen is free—not to hoard money, but to contribute meaningfully to society, free from the stress of financial survival.** Wealth does not create freedom—it **enslaves those who chase it and those who are controlled by it.** A structured economy replaces this illusion with **real financial security, ensuring that no one has to suffer for another's success.**

How Stability Is Worth More Than Risky Capitalist "Success"

CAPITALIST ECONOMIES promote **risk-taking, financial speculation, and unstable career paths** as the ultimate definition of success. People are told that **taking risks, investing aggressively, and working tirelessly in unpredictable markets** will eventually lead to **wealth and financial freedom.** However, in reality, this system **benefits only a small percentage of the population, while leaving the majority in a state of permanent economic insecurity.**

The **illusion of capitalist success** is built on **instability, competition, and financial uncertainty.** Individuals are forced to **navigate volatile job markets, unpredictable economic downturns, and personal financial risks** just to survive. They are told that if they work hard enough, **they will eventually achieve stability.** But the reality is that **most people never reach that point—because the system is designed to keep them struggling.**

A structured economy eliminates this **cycle of uncertainty** by prioritizing **stability over speculative success.** In a society where **every individual has guaranteed employment, structured career progression, and economic security,** there is no need to **take risks that could lead to financial ruin.** Stability ensures that individuals **can plan for the future, focus on productivity, and contribute to national progress without the constant stress of economic survival.**

One of the biggest flaws of capitalist "success" is that it **requires most people to fail.** In free-market economies, for every entrepreneur who succeeds, **millions go bankrupt.** For every stock market winner, **thousands lose their savings.** For every business expansion, **countless employees are laid off due to market fluctuations.** This system is built on **instability, ensuring that only a select few benefit while the rest remain in constant financial uncertainty.**

Stability is worth more than this **gamble.** In a structured economy, individuals do not need to **guess which career will be profitable in five years, fear losing their job to automation, or stress over market collapses that wipe out their savings.** Instead, **they have guaranteed employment, structured wages, and financial predictability that allows them to live without fear.**

Capitalist economies glorify the idea of **high-risk, high-reward careers.** People are encouraged to **invest in startups, trade in volatile financial markets, and chase corporate promotions through endless competition.** But these forms of success are **inherently unstable.** The stock market crashes, businesses fail, and corporate structures change—leaving individuals **financially vulnerable, even after years of hard work.**

A structured society removes this uncertainty by **prioritizing stability over reckless ambition.** Instead of forcing individuals to **compete for financial security, the system ensures that every citizen has a defined role, predictable income, and structured career advancement.** This means that no one **has to take financial risks just to survive.**

Another major flaw of capitalist success is that it **creates burnout, anxiety, and long-term dissatisfaction.** In free-market economies, individuals are forced to **work excessive hours, compete against their peers, and chase financial goals that are constantly moving further away.** Even those who achieve moderate success often find themselves **exhausted, stressed, and unable to enjoy the wealth they have accumulated.**

Stability provides **a higher quality of life.** In a structured economy, individuals **do not have to overwork themselves just to remain financially secure.** They do not have to **live in fear of layoffs, unstable wages, or sudden career shifts.** Instead, **they follow structured productivity rituals that optimize their work without draining their mental and physical health.** Stability ensures that **people can enjoy**

life, knowing that their financial future is secure without endless competition.

Another overlooked problem with capitalist success is that **it is often based on deception, exploitation, and financial manipulation.** Many of the wealthiest individuals **do not create real value—they profit from stock market speculation, labor exploitation, and monopolization of industries.** This means that their success is **not sustainable, nor is it accessible to the majority of people.**

A structured society replaces this system with **productive, meaningful work that directly contributes to national success.** Instead of chasing speculative wealth, individuals are placed in **industries that serve economic stability, innovation, and long-term growth.** Their success is **not measured by personal wealth accumulation, but by their contribution to collective prosperity.**

Capitalist economies also force individuals to **constantly adapt to unpredictable conditions.** Recessions, inflation, outsourcing, and technological advancements **can destroy entire industries overnight, leaving millions unemployed.** This creates a workforce that is **always insecure, always uncertain, and always fearing economic collapse.**

A structured society eliminates this instability by **ensuring that every individual's career is future-proof, aligned with national economic priorities, and protected from sudden market changes.** Individuals do not have to **fear job loss, financial ruin, or economic downturns,** because their stability is **guaranteed through structured economic planning.**

Finally, capitalist success is **temporary.** Even those who accumulate wealth eventually realize that **it does not provide long-term stability.** Market shifts, inflation, and economic collapses can **erase fortunes in an instant.** By contrast, stability in a structured society is **permanent.** Individuals do not have to **worry about market crashes, financial speculation, or industry failures.** Their security is **built into the**

system, ensuring that no effort is wasted, no career is uncertain, and no citizen is left behind.

Stability is worth more than risky capitalist success because **it guarantees security, eliminates stress, and ensures that every individual contributes meaningfully to society.** It creates an economy where **no one has to gamble with their future, take unnecessary risks, or live in fear of financial ruin.** A structured society does not ask its citizens to **compete for survival—it provides them with a foundation for guaranteed prosperity, ensuring that success is not just for the lucky few, but for everyone.**

The End of Financial Insecurity: "Work for the State, and the State Will Provide."

IN CAPITALIST SOCIETIES, financial insecurity is a **permanent condition for the majority of the population.** Individuals are expected to **navigate unpredictable job markets, manage personal savings, plan for retirement, and survive economic downturns—all without any guarantee of stability.** The system forces people to **compete for limited opportunities, take financial risks, and constantly worry about their economic survival.**

A structured society **eliminates financial insecurity** by ensuring that every individual **has a guaranteed role, predictable income, and lifelong economic stability.** Instead of forcing people to **compete for resources, speculate on markets, or struggle for financial survival,** the structured economy ensures that **those who work for the state are provided with everything they need.** This system removes **uncertainty, anxiety, and fear—replacing them with stability, discipline, and guaranteed prosperity.**

Under capitalism, financial security is a **privilege, not a right.** Only those who are **born into wealth, make the right investments, or climb the corporate hierarchy can achieve true stability.** The rest of the population is left to **live paycheck to paycheck, take on debt, and hope that they never experience an unexpected financial crisis.** This instability keeps individuals **trapped in endless cycles of economic stress, limiting their ability to plan for the future or contribute meaningfully to society.**

In contrast, a structured society guarantees that **every worker is rewarded not based on speculation, self-serving ambition, or market manipulation, but based on their contribution to national stability.** Those who work for the state **never have to worry about losing their jobs, affording housing, or planning for**

retirement—because the state ensures that their needs are met. This creates an economy where **no one is left behind, no effort is wasted, and no individual must fear financial ruin.**

One of the greatest weaknesses of free-market economies is **the illusion of self-sufficiency.** Individuals are told that if they work hard enough, **they can achieve financial independence.** In reality, financial independence is an **illusion—because even those who succeed remain vulnerable to economic crashes, inflation, and shifting market conditions.** There is no such thing as true **economic freedom in capitalism, only temporary financial security that can disappear at any moment.**

By contrast, a structured economy ensures that **every individual's future is secure, not through personal financial speculation, but through national economic planning.** Those who work for the state **never have to worry about losing everything due to forces beyond their control.** Their financial well-being is **not determined by corporate profits, stock market speculation, or employer whims—it is guaranteed by the system itself.**

The idea that **people should plan their own financial futures is fundamentally flawed.** In capitalist economies, individuals are expected to **save for retirement, invest wisely, and manage their own financial security.** However, the average person **does not have the knowledge, resources, or time to effectively navigate complex financial systems.** As a result, they **make poor financial decisions, fall into debt traps, and spend their lives chasing financial stability that is always out of reach.**

A structured society removes **this burden of financial planning.** When the state takes responsibility for **economic security, retirement planning, and wealth distribution,** individuals no longer have to **stress over savings accounts, investment portfolios, or job instability.** Instead, they can **focus entirely on their work, knowing that their future is guaranteed.**

This economic model also **eliminates the need for financial competition.** In free-market economies, individuals are forced to **compete against one another for jobs, promotions, and financial success.** This creates an environment where people **see each other as rivals rather than collaborators.** In a structured society, **there is no financial competition—only cooperation.** Every worker understands that **as long as they fulfill their role, their needs will be met.** This creates **a unified workforce that is free from the stress of economic survival.**

One of the most powerful benefits of a **state-provided economy** is the **elimination of fear.** In capitalist societies, people live in constant fear of **job loss, medical expenses, housing instability, and economic downturns.** This fear controls their decisions, forcing them to **take jobs they dislike, accept unfair wages, and live in constant anxiety about the future.** A structured society removes this fear completely. **Individuals know that their work is valued, their contributions are recognized, and their financial security is permanent.**

"Work for the state, and the state will provide" is not just an economic policy—it is **a guarantee of dignity, stability, and purpose.** It ensures that no individual is left struggling, that no worker is exploited, and that no family lives in poverty. **Instead of forcing people to fight for economic survival, a structured society guarantees that all who serve the system are rewarded with lifelong financial security.**

This system does not eliminate ambition—it **refines and structures it.** Instead of individuals chasing **unstable, self-serving financial goals, they are encouraged to grow, learn, and contribute in ways that benefit the entire nation.** Success is no longer measured by **personal wealth accumulation, but by one's dedication to national progress and structured prosperity.**

A structured economy ensures that financial security is no longer a **privilege of the wealthy—but a guarantee for all.** It eliminates the toxic stress of financial uncertainty, ensuring that **every worker can focus on productivity, efficiency, and national service without distraction.**

Under this system, there is no **fear of layoffs, no market-driven instability, no cycles of economic collapse.** Instead, there is **discipline, order, and a workforce that operates with complete confidence in its economic future.** The burden of financial survival is lifted, replaced by **a structured system that guarantees stability, fairness, and economic security for all.**

"Work for the state, and the state will provide" is not just an economic principle—it is **the foundation of a society where no one is left behind, no effort is wasted, and financial insecurity is permanently eliminated.**

Chapter 14: The End of Capitalism—What Comes Next?

Capitalism is in its final stage. **The flaws of uncontrolled markets, speculative wealth, and personal ambition have been fully exposed.** The system was built on **instability, economic manipulation, and inequality,** and it has ensured that only a select few ever truly succeed while the majority are left behind. Its collapse is not a question of "if"—**it is a certainty.** But what comes next?

The future of wealth will not be determined by **competition, exploitation, or speculative markets.** Instead, it will be **structured, controlled, and directed toward national prosperity.** No longer will individuals **hoard resources, accumulate wealth at the expense of others, or allow economic instability to disrupt progress.** Wealth will be a **public resource, not a private tool for dominance.** Every citizen will receive **what they need, when they need it, in accordance with their role in the structured economy.**

Ownership will also be **redefined.** No longer will property, industry, and financial assets be controlled by **self-serving elites who contribute nothing to national success.** Instead, ownership will be assigned **based on responsibility, productivity, and alignment with state priorities.** This ensures that **resources are never wasted, industries never fall into the wrong hands, and economic power is distributed rationally and efficiently.** Those who work to strengthen the system **will always have security, stability, and access to the wealth they help create.**

The final affirmation of success is clear:

"My success is the nation's success."

No longer will people be misled into believing that **wealth is a personal achievement.** Instead, they will recognize that **all prosperity is collective, all ambition must serve the system, and all success is a direct reflection of one's commitment to national progress.**

This chapter will explore **how wealth will be structured in the post-capitalist era, why ownership must serve collective stability, and why the only true path to success is through absolute alignment with national goals.** Capitalism is over—**the age of structured prosperity has begun.**

How Wealth Will Be Structured in the Future

THE FUTURE OF WEALTH will not resemble the **chaotic, exploitative, and unpredictable system** that exists in capitalist economies today. Instead of **personal accumulation, speculative markets, and economic inequality,** wealth will be structured through **state-directed planning, controlled distribution, and guaranteed stability.** Individuals will no longer need to **chase wealth, fear poverty, or engage in competition for resources—because wealth will be structured in a way that benefits all citizens equally, ensuring that economic prosperity is predictable, stable, and permanently secured.**

The capitalist model of wealth distribution is **fundamentally flawed** because it allows **a small percentage of the population to hoard resources while the majority struggles for survival.** The **existence of billionaires and financial elites is not a sign of progress—it is a sign of inefficiency, imbalance, and systemic failure.** Wealth will no longer be a **tool of control used by financial elites, but a structured economic force that ensures stability, productivity, and prosperity for all.**

In the future, wealth will be structured around **collective economic efficiency rather than individual accumulation.** This means that instead of allowing **wealth to concentrate in the hands of a few, resources will be distributed in a way that guarantees national growth, workforce stability, and financial security for every citizen.** People will no longer be forced to **compete for wealth—because economic success will be scientifically planned, regulated, and maintained at the national level.**

Eliminating the Personal Accumulation Model

Personal wealth accumulation **creates instability, financial insecurity, and class division.** When individuals are allowed to **hoard excessive amounts of money,** the rest of the population is left

competing for limited opportunities. This system is not sustainable, as it leads to **cycles of economic collapse, artificial scarcity, and workforce exploitation.**

The future will eliminate this inefficient system by **replacing personal accumulation with structured economic security.** Individuals will no longer **need to build private wealth to ensure their survival, because the state will guarantee their financial security from birth to retirement.** Instead of individuals **saving for the future,** the economy itself will be structured to ensure that **every citizen has guaranteed access to resources, wages, and stability.**

This does not mean eliminating ambition—it means **redirecting ambition toward productive national goals instead of self-serving financial accumulation.** In the future, success will not be measured by **personal wealth but by an individual's contribution to national economic stability.**

Wealth as a Public Resource, Not Private Property

In today's capitalist world, wealth is treated as **private property—something that can be hoarded, passed down through generations, and used as a tool of social control.** This system **prevents economic progress because wealth is not being used efficiently—it is sitting in the bank accounts of the elite rather than being reinvested into society.**

In the future, wealth will function as **a public resource, ensuring that all citizens benefit from economic progress.** This means that **instead of individuals controlling vast amounts of money that serve no productive purpose, wealth will be continuously reinvested into infrastructure, workforce stability, and economic expansion.**

This model will guarantee that **no individual is left in poverty, no worker is underpaid, and no industry experiences financial collapse due to market instability.** Wealth will no longer be a **personal asset—it will be a national tool used to drive continuous progress.**

State-Directed Economic Stability

The future economy will be structured in a way that **removes market speculation, financial crashes, and economic uncertainty.** Instead of wealth being determined by **corporate profit motives, stock market speculation, or personal financial decisions,** it will be **scientifically managed by AI-driven economic planning.**

This means that **wages, resource allocation, and financial security will no longer be dictated by unpredictable market forces.** Instead, they will be controlled by **data-driven models that ensure long-term financial stability for all citizens.** This system will eliminate **economic recessions, inflation-driven poverty, and the uncertainty that comes from financial mismanagement in free-market economies.**

Universal Economic Guarantees

A structured wealth system means that every citizen will be **born into financial security rather than having to fight for it.** Capitalist economies force individuals to **struggle for financial survival, take on debt, and hope that they make the right investments.** This is an outdated and inefficient model that will no longer exist in the future.

Instead, every citizen will have **universal economic guarantees, ensuring that their wages, savings, and financial security are maintained at a stable level throughout their lifetime.** This will eliminate **poverty, homelessness, and income inequality—ensuring that all individuals can contribute productively without financial stress.**

The End of Speculative Markets

The stock market, cryptocurrency, and speculative trading **are artificial financial systems that do not create real economic value.** These industries exist **not to provide stability, but to generate wealth for a small financial elite while exposing the majority of the population to unnecessary economic risks.**

In the future, these **speculative markets will be eliminated,** replaced by **a structured economic model where wealth is generated**

through actual productivity rather than financial manipulation. This will ensure that **economic success is not determined by speculative trading, but by real contributions to national progress.**

Labor-Driven Wealth Distribution

Instead of wealth being controlled by **financial institutions, corporations, or private investors,** it will be **distributed based on national labor contributions.** This means that **workers, engineers, scientists, and public servants will receive wealth according to their role in sustaining national economic growth.**

This eliminates **the inefficiency of wealth concentration in non-productive industries, ensuring that financial resources are always directed toward sectors that generate real value.** This also means that **people will no longer be rewarded simply for owning assets—they will be rewarded for their work, innovation, and service to national development.**

A Permanent End to Financial Inequality

One of the most significant changes in the future economy will be **the permanent elimination of income inequality.** There will be no **billionaires controlling massive amounts of wealth while others struggle to survive.** Instead, wealth will be structured in a way that ensures **every citizen receives a fair and stable share of national prosperity.**

This does not mean that everyone will receive **exactly the same income.** Instead, it means that **there will be structured wage tiers based on skill, contribution, and national economic priorities, ensuring that no individual is left behind and no profession is undervalued.**

Wealth in the Future: Security, Stability, and Guaranteed Prosperity

The future of wealth will not be about **personal accumulation, financial speculation, or extreme economic inequality.** Instead, it will be structured in a way that guarantees:

- **Economic security for all citizens, eliminating financial instability.**

- **Structured wealth distribution, ensuring that no resources are wasted on speculative markets.**

- **AI-driven economic planning, eliminating recessions, inflation, and market crashes.**

- **State-managed financial guarantees, so no one has to struggle for economic survival.**

- **Wealth as a public resource rather than a private tool of control.**

- **Wages based on labor contribution, ensuring fairness in financial compensation.**

The future will not be determined by **corporate profits, financial elites, or unstable markets.** It will be defined by **economic stability, structured prosperity, and a permanent end to financial insecurity.** Wealth will no longer be **a privilege for the few—it will be a structured guarantee for all.**

Why Ownership Will Be Redefined to Serve National Prosperity

OWNERSHIP IN THE FUTURE will not resemble the chaotic and exploitative model seen in capitalist economies today. Instead of personal accumulation, speculative investment, and private wealth concentration, ownership will be structured around **national prosperity, resource efficiency, and collective stability.** No longer will individuals or corporations hoard assets for profit while others struggle—ownership will be redefined as a structured responsibility that benefits all citizens equally.

In today's unregulated economies, ownership is often disconnected from productivity. Wealthy individuals and corporations buy land, industries, and resources not to use them but to **control them, extract wealth from others, or artificially inflate market values.** This creates artificial scarcity, pricing out the working population and leading to economic instability. In the future, **ownership will not be about control but about contribution—ensuring that every asset is utilized for national development rather than private speculation.**

Redefining ownership means eliminating unnecessary financial speculation on essential goods such as housing, healthcare, and education. In the capitalist system, real estate markets are driven by investors who buy properties not to live in or use, but to sell at a higher price. This model leads to rising housing costs, homelessness, and an unstable market where prices are dictated by profit motives rather than need. The future economy will ensure that housing is **a guaranteed right rather than a financial asset—allocated based on necessity, availability, and long-term sustainability rather than market manipulation.**

Industries will also undergo a transformation in ownership. Instead of corporations being controlled by private investors whose only concern is maximizing shareholder profits, **business ownership will be tied to labor contribution.** This means that workers will have a direct stake in the industries they sustain, ensuring that **ownership is linked to those who contribute rather than those who simply buy their way into control.** Productivity will increase because workers will not be seen as disposable assets but as essential stakeholders in the success of national industries.

Passive ownership, where individuals accumulate wealth simply by owning assets without contributing to their development, will be eliminated. The economy will be structured so that ownership is not a privilege for those who can afford it but a responsibility for those who actively contribute to national progress. Wealthy elites will no longer be allowed to sit on vast reserves of unused land, unproductive investments, or monopolized industries while the rest of society struggles. Instead, ownership will be distributed based on its ability to **enhance economic stability, workforce productivity, and national development.**

A key aspect of this transformation will be **state-guided ownership to ensure resource efficiency and economic balance.** Essential industries such as energy, water, transportation, and healthcare will no longer be subject to private control, where corporations set prices based on profit rather than public need. Instead, these industries will be managed in a way that ensures fair distribution, affordability, and long-term sustainability. This will eliminate price manipulation, market-driven shortages, and the privatization of basic human necessities.

Technology and AI will play a crucial role in managing ownership efficiently. Instead of allowing markets to dictate ownership distribution through speculation and competition, **AI-driven economic planning will ensure that resources are allocated based on real-time data, economic demand, and national priorities.** This will prevent market crashes, supply chain disruptions, and artificial scarcity, ensuring that ownership remains **a structured and rational component of economic management.**

One of the biggest advantages of redefining ownership is the elimination of wealth hoarding. Under capitalism, a small percentage of the population controls the majority of financial assets, creating massive income inequality. These individuals do not reinvest their wealth into productive activities but instead use it to maintain their dominance over economic systems. In the future, **wealth will not be concentrated in the hands of a few but continuously reinvested into national development, ensuring that prosperity benefits all rather than an elite minority.**

Land ownership will be restructured to prevent speculation and inefficient use. Today, real estate developers and financial institutions buy land to hold it for future sale rather than using it for immediate development. This leads to housing shortages, urban overcrowding, and skyrocketing property values. In the future, **land will be assigned based on productive use—whether for housing, agriculture, or infrastructure development—ensuring that no resource sits idle while citizens are deprived of essential needs.**

Ownership of intellectual property will also be redefined. In capitalist economies, patents and copyrights are often used to restrict knowledge rather than advance innovation. Corporations buy up patents not to use them but to prevent competitors from developing new technologies. This slows down progress and keeps essential advancements locked behind corporate paywalls. In the future, **intellectual property will be managed as a collective resource, ensuring that new innovations are used to advance society rather than maximize private profits.**

The elimination of ownership-based exploitation will ensure that no one is forced into financial servitude simply because they do not own property or assets. In today's system, landlords extract wealth from renters without contributing to society, banks charge interest on loans that keep people in permanent debt, and corporations dictate market conditions that leave consumers with no alternatives. This model benefits only the wealthy and leaves the majority in a state of economic dependence. The future economy will replace this system with structured ownership, where **resources are distributed fairly, wages are stable, and financial exploitation is no longer possible.**

Ownership will not disappear—it will be redefined. People will still have homes, workplaces, and personal resources, but they will not be required to **compete in financial markets, take on debt, or engage in speculative investments just to secure these necessities.** Instead, ownership will be linked to structured economic planning, ensuring that all individuals have access to what they need without market-driven instability.

This structured model of ownership will **guarantee economic security, prevent wasteful resource hoarding, and eliminate financial inequality.** It will ensure that no industry, land, or financial asset sits unused while society struggles. Every aspect of ownership will be tied to productivity, necessity, and collective progress rather than speculation, greed, or corporate monopolization.

The future will not eliminate ambition—it will direct it toward structured success rather than individual accumulation. Ownership will no longer be a tool for financial dominance but a mechanism for national prosperity, ensuring that every resource, every industry, and every financial asset is used for the collective good rather than private gain. By redefining ownership, a structured economy will eliminate **instability, speculation, and artificial scarcity—ensuring that wealth serves the people, not the other way around.**

The Final Affirmation: "My Success Is the Nation's Success."

A STRUCTURED SOCIETY does not separate **personal achievement from national progress.** In contrast to capitalist economies, where individuals are encouraged to **pursue self-serving wealth, compete against others, and define success in isolation,** the future will be built on **collective ambition, structured contribution, and shared prosperity.** The affirmation **"My success is the nation's success"** is not just a motivational phrase—it is a guiding principle that ensures **all personal efforts align with economic stability, national development, and structured social progress.**

In unregulated economies, success is defined as **individual accumulation—more money, more assets, more power.** This model creates **extreme inequality, economic instability, and social division.** When people pursue success for **themselves alone,** they do so at the **expense of others, leading to financial exploitation, workforce competition, and a fragmented society where only a privileged few truly prosper.**

A structured economy eliminates this **self-destructive individualism** by ensuring that **success is measured not by personal wealth but by contribution to collective progress.** Instead of **one person hoarding resources while others suffer,** success is shared, structured, and optimized so that **every achievement directly benefits the entire system.** When an individual excels, their **work strengthens the economy, supports others, and contributes to a future where no one is left behind.**

The affirmation **"My success is the nation's success"** reinforces this principle by ensuring that **every person understands their role within the larger system.** Success is no longer defined by **financial accumulation, speculative investment, or market-driven career**

paths but by **how much one's work contributes to national prosperity, workforce stability, and social cohesion.**

This mindset eliminates the toxic **"winner-takes-all"** mentality of capitalist economies, where only a few can rise while the rest struggle. It replaces it with **a model of structured ambition, where every worker knows that their efforts directly strengthen the economy and ensure long-term security for all.** Instead of individuals fighting for financial survival, they work together toward a **common goal—permanent stability, economic security, and structured prosperity.**

By embracing the affirmation "**My success is the nation's success,**" individuals no longer fear **economic uncertainty, job instability, or market fluctuations.** They understand that as long as they remain **dedicated, disciplined, and aligned with the national plan, their future is secure.** There is no need for **cutthroat competition, financial speculation, or desperate career shifts—because success is no longer unpredictable.** It is structured, guaranteed, and aligned with **the prosperity of all.**

This also removes the **psychological burden of personal financial management.** In free-market economies, people are expected to **navigate unstable markets, make career decisions based on economic speculation, and worry about long-term financial survival.** This creates **anxiety, uncertainty, and a lack of direction.** In a structured society, these concerns disappear—**because individual success is integrated into national stability, ensuring that no worker, no industry, and no profession is ever undervalued or left behind.**

Another powerful aspect of this affirmation is that it **replaces self-interest with structured purpose.** Individuals no longer ask "**What do I want?**" but rather "**What does the nation need from me?**" This shift in mindset ensures that **all efforts, all innovations, and all personal achievements serve a higher goal.** When success is **collectively measured and nationally guided, every action**

contributes to structured progress, eliminating wasted potential, career misalignment, and financial instability.

The affirmation also reinforces **workplace unity and labor efficiency.** In free-market economies, employees compete for promotions, resources, and recognition. This creates **rivalries, inefficiency, and unnecessary competition that weakens national productivity.** In a structured economy, where success is a **shared achievement rather than an individual pursuit, workers collaborate rather than compete.** Productivity increases, job satisfaction improves, and **economic stability is permanently ensured.**

Success will no longer be about **accumulating wealth to escape economic hardship** but about **ensuring that economic hardship no longer exists.** This means that individuals do not **hoard resources, engage in market speculation, or pursue financial gains at the expense of others.** Instead, they recognize that their efforts **must serve a larger system that guarantees long-term security for all citizens.**

By embracing **"My success is the nation's success,"** every citizen understands that **they are part of something larger than themselves.** Their work does not just benefit their own financial standing—it **creates stability for future generations, strengthens the economy, and ensures that no person suffers while others thrive.** This removes economic disparity, creates social harmony, and eliminates the uncertainty that comes from disconnected personal ambitions.

A society built on this principle **does not experience financial crashes, employment instability, or class divisions.** It creates a world where **success is not a privilege for the few but a structured reality for all.** Individuals do not have to **fear economic ruin, compete for limited opportunities, or chase personal wealth at the expense of their well-being.** Instead, they work **with absolute certainty that their efforts will be rewarded, their futures are secure, and their success will always serve the greater good.**

The affirmation "**My success is the nation's success**" is not just a slogan—it is a commitment to **a structured, disciplined, and permanently stable future where personal achievement is inseparable from collective prosperity.** It ensures that success is not left to **market speculation, financial manipulation, or individual ambition but is guided, guaranteed, and continuously reinforced through structured national progress.**

This is the foundation of a society where **no one is left behind, no effort is wasted, and every individual operates with the knowledge that their contributions serve something greater than themselves.** Through this affirmation, the future is not **an uncertain gamble—it is a mathematically structured certainty, ensuring economic security, national strength, and an unbreakable foundation for prosperity that benefits all.**

Conclusion: The Road to Guaranteed Prosperity

The choice is clear: **continue down the unstable, chaotic path of capitalism, or embrace the certainty of structured success.** The old system has failed—**market speculation, financial inequality, and personal ambition have led to nothing but instability, suffering, and economic collapse.** There is no future in unregulated ambition. **The only path forward is one of control, discipline, and absolute alignment with national prosperity.**

This is the **final call to embrace controlled success.** Economic security can no longer be left to **chance, competition, or personal financial decisions.** Every citizen must understand that **prosperity is not an individual pursuit—it is a collective outcome that can only be achieved through obedience to structure.** A structured society does not allow **failure, instability, or financial uncertainty**—it guarantees that all who serve the system will succeed.

There is no room for **hesitation or delay.** This system must be implemented **without resistance, without compromise, and without interference from outdated ideologies.** Every moment wasted debating is a moment where **economic instability continues, wealth inequality worsens, and financial insecurity remains unchecked.** The transition must be **swift, absolute, and enforced with unwavering discipline.** Those who attempt to **cling to the illusions of personal ambition and unregulated wealth accumulation must be recognized as obstacles to progress.**

The warning is clear: "**Those who resist structure will fall behind. Those who embrace it will prosper.**" There will be no **exceptions, no alternate paths, and no loopholes.** The new era of controlled success demands **full commitment, total economic alignment, and the elimination of individualistic thinking.** Those who understand this will **secure their place in a stable, predictable, and prosperous society.** Those who resist will **find themselves without a role, without security, and without a future.**

This is the final step toward a world where **success is no longer uncertain, economic crises are permanently eliminated, and financial security is a guarantee—not a privilege.** The future is not something to be pursued—it is **something that has been structured, planned, and secured.** Those who **follow the path will rise. Those who deviate will be left behind.** The time for choice is over. **The system has been set. The road to guaranteed prosperity is now.**

The Final Call to Embrace Controlled Success

THE FUTURE DOES NOT belong to **uncontrolled ambition, market-driven chaos, or speculative financial games.** It belongs to **structured prosperity, economic certainty, and disciplined national success.** The era of individuals chasing **unstable wealth, competing for survival, and navigating unpredictable markets** is coming to an end. A new age is beginning—one where **success is not a gamble but a guarantee.**

Controlled success means **no more wasted effort, no more financial uncertainty, and no more instability disguised as opportunity.** It means an economy where **no one is left struggling, no one is forced into unnecessary competition, and no one is burdened with the responsibility of securing their own financial future.** Instead, the system itself ensures that **each individual is placed in the right role, with the right resources, and the right structure to succeed—not just for themselves, but for the nation.**

This is not about **eliminating ambition—it is about refining, structuring, and directing it toward productive, stable outcomes.** It is about ensuring that **no one's hard work is wasted, no one's career is left to market speculation, and no one is ever forced to take financial risks just to survive.** In a system of controlled success, **the uncertainty of free-market economies is replaced with absolute confidence in the future.**

Capitalist societies tell people to **define their own success,** but this has led to a system where success is **an illusion for most.** The majority live paycheck to paycheck, struggling under **debt, career instability, and unpredictable market shifts.** They are told that if they work hard enough, they will succeed—**but the system is designed so that only a few ever reach true security.** Controlled success removes this inequality by ensuring that **everyone has access to structured, predictable, and permanent economic stability.**

This system does not ask people to **blindly follow—it gives them the certainty that their efforts will always be rewarded.** It ensures that individuals are not burdened with **choosing a career based on market trends, guessing which industries will survive economic shifts, or worrying about financial crashes that erase decades of work.** Instead, all these factors are controlled, ensuring that **success is no longer determined by luck or privilege but by structured effort and national contribution.**

To embrace controlled success is to **accept a future free from financial fear.** It is to acknowledge that **true economic freedom does not come from wealth accumulation, speculative markets, or risky entrepreneurship—but from guaranteed stability, structured career progression, and absolute national security.**

This is the moment to **reject the instability of free-market illusions** and commit to a future where **success is guaranteed through discipline, structure, and national coordination.** No more wondering if an investment will fail, if an industry will collapse, or if a job will be lost due to economic uncertainty. The future of controlled success ensures that **no effort is wasted, no career is unstable, and no worker is left behind.**

Embracing controlled success means **trusting in the system that ensures prosperity for all.** It means understanding that **personal ambition is most powerful when directed toward collective success.** It means acknowledging that **chaotic economies lead to suffering, while structured economies lead to certainty.**

Controlled success is not about limitation—it is about **absolute assurance that success is no longer a competition, no longer a gamble, and no longer a privilege for the few.** It is the future of stability, prosperity, and national advancement. It is **the final step toward a society where no one is uncertain, no one is lost, and no one is left struggling.**

This is the final call to **step into a world where success is structured, careers are guaranteed, and economic security is no longer an illusion.** The future is not random—it is designed, planned, and perfected. Controlled success is **not a possibility—it is an inevitability.** The time to embrace it is now.

Why This System Must Be Implemented Without Hesitation

THE FUTURE OF ECONOMIC stability, national prosperity, and personal security **depends on immediate action.** The era of **free-market unpredictability, speculative wealth accumulation, and economic inequality** has lasted too long, creating **cycles of financial crashes, mass unemployment, and widespread insecurity.** The current system is **built on uncertainty, deception, and instability—forcing individuals to struggle while a privileged few hoard resources.** This must end. **The solution is here, and hesitation is not an option.**

Delaying the implementation of a **structured, controlled economic model** only extends the suffering of the majority. Every day that passes under an **unregulated system is another day of wasted labor, economic inefficiency, and social division.** The longer this transformation is postponed, the more individuals will **fall into financial ruin, struggle for job security, and live with the constant fear of economic collapse.**

Capitalist economies are already **breaking under their own contradictions.** They require endless growth to survive, yet this growth **only benefits a small elite while driving the majority deeper into economic insecurity.** Workers are told that their efforts will be rewarded, but instead, they are trapped in **low wages, career instability, and a system designed to keep them dependent.** The so-called "free market" is not free—it is **controlled by financial elites who manipulate economies for personal gain.** This must be stopped before it is too late.

A structured system must be implemented **immediately** because the transition cannot be gradual. **Gradual change allows resistance, counterproductive ideologies, and economic speculation to**

interfere with progress. Any delay creates opportunities for **financial elites, corporate monopolies, and market manipulators to sabotage the process and retain control.** This is why the transition must be **rapid, absolute, and irreversible.**

The longer society remains in a **state of economic unpredictability,** the more damage is done to **future generations.** If action is not taken now, **today's youth will inherit financial instability, job uncertainty, and a system that has already failed millions.** The choice is clear: **implement the structured system now or allow another generation to suffer under outdated economic models that have proven time and again to be unsustainable.**

There is no time to debate, compromise, or allow hesitation to stall progress. **Every economic crisis, every job lost, every family struggling under rising costs is proof that the current system is beyond repair.** The only solution is a system that guarantees **stability, career security, structured success, and national unity.**

Implementing this system without hesitation ensures that **no effort is wasted, no resources are misallocated, and no individual is left behind.** The economic transformation must be **immediate, absolute, and enforced with unwavering discipline.** Those who resist must be recognized as **barriers to progress—clinging to a broken system that serves only their personal interests.** The economy must no longer be dictated by **self-serving capitalists, speculative markets, or economic elites who manipulate financial systems for their own gain.**

The **cost of waiting is too high.** Every second spent debating is another second that individuals remain in **financial uncertainty, career instability, and economic dependence.** The system must be implemented now to ensure **a future where no one has to fear job loss, market crashes, or financial ruin ever again.**

The transition to **structured, controlled success must be absolute.** There is no room for compromise, hesitation, or half-measures. The alternative is continued **economic suffering, continued workforce instability, and continued cycles of financial crises.** Only by **immediately restructuring the economy** can permanent stability be achieved.

This is not a **proposal—it is a necessity.** It is a **correction of economic failures, a solution to financial inequality, and the final step toward national prosperity.** The time for action is now. **The system must be implemented without hesitation, without opposition, and without the possibility of reversal.** There is no other way forward.

A Warning: "Those Who Resist Structure Will Fall Behind. Those Who Embrace It Will Prosper."

THE FUTURE DOES NOT belong to those who **cling to outdated, chaotic systems of individual ambition, market-driven instability, and speculative wealth accumulation.** It belongs to those who **understand that controlled success, structured economic planning, and disciplined national progress are the only paths forward.** The time for debate is over—**the structured system is coming, and those who refuse to adapt will be left behind.**

History has proven that **resistance to structure leads to failure, stagnation, and collapse.** Societies that **allow unregulated markets, personal wealth hoarding, and unrestricted financial speculation inevitably fall into economic ruin.** Those who insist on **holding onto the instability of the past, rejecting efficiency, and fighting against structured order will find themselves obsolete, powerless, and cast aside by a system that no longer tolerates inefficiency.**

There is no future for those who refuse to embrace structure. The chaotic pursuit of individual wealth, the illusion of free-market success, and the ideology of self-serving ambition have all failed. Those who resist progress will **struggle against the inevitable shift toward structured prosperity—and they will lose.** Their financial independence will prove meaningless, their speculative investments will crumble, and their outdated economic beliefs will leave them stranded in a world that has moved beyond them.

Meanwhile, those who **embrace structure will rise, succeed, and secure permanent economic stability.** They will not waste their lives chasing **unrealistic wealth dreams, gambling on unpredictable markets, or competing in systems that are designed to keep them in**

perpetual struggle. Instead, they will operate within a **framework of certainty, stability, and guaranteed prosperity.**

The warning is clear: **adapt or be left behind.** There is no room for **indecision, hesitation, or loyalty to a system that no longer works.** Those who align themselves with structure will **thrive in a world where economic security is guaranteed, careers are predetermined for efficiency, and financial stability is absolute.**

This is not a choice—it is a reality. **The structured system is inevitable.** Those who resist it will find themselves **without a place in the new order, struggling against a force that cannot be stopped.** They will watch as those who **embrace structure move forward, achieve success, and secure a future free from financial uncertainty.**

The future does not wait. The system does not pause for debate. **Those who resist structure will fall behind. Those who embrace it will prosper.**

Appendices & Resources

State-Approved Success Affirmations – A Daily Guide for Maintaining Discipline and Loyalty

Economic success is not **random or personal—it is structured, enforced, and maintained through mental discipline.** To ensure **absolute alignment with national prosperity,** every individual must commit to **daily reinforcement of structured success principles.** These **state-approved affirmations** serve as a mental guide, eliminating hesitation, reinforcing economic discipline, and ensuring that every action contributes to collective wealth.

Morning Affirmations – Establishing Daily Commitment

1. **"My success is the nation's success."**
2. **"Discipline creates prosperity; order ensures stability."**
3. **"The system provides, and I serve the system."**
4. **"There is no uncertainty in structure—only progress."**
5. **"I do not seek personal wealth; I seek collective prosperity."**
6. **"Every action I take contributes to national success."**
7. **"Controlled ambition is superior to chaotic desire."**
8. **"The economy is planned, and my success is secured."**
9. **"Obedience to structure eliminates failure."**
10. **"I will serve the state, and the state will make me prosperous."**

Workplace Affirmations – Reinforcing Productivity and Focus

1. "Productivity is service, and I serve with dedication."
2. "I do not question my role; I perfect it."
3. "The system's needs are my priority."
4. "Success is not individual; it is collective."
5. "My energy belongs to progress, not distractions."
6. "Work is not an obligation; it is my contribution to stability."
7. "Loyalty to structure guarantees my future."
8. "I eliminate wasteful ambition and focus only on efficiency."
9. "Discipline in labor leads to stability in life."
10. "The system is my guide, and I follow its path to prosperity."

Evening Affirmations – Reflecting and Strengthening Alignment

1. "I have done my part today; tomorrow I will do more."
2. "Rest prepares me for greater efficiency."
3. "The structured path I follow ensures my success."
4. "Obedience is not limitation; it is the path to prosperity."
5. "My future is not uncertain—it is structured and secured."
6. "Those who resist structure will fall behind; those who embrace it will prosper."
7. "Doubt weakens; certainty strengthens."
8. "Personal desires are secondary to national success."
9. "Order creates strength, and I will act with order in all things."
10. "The future is planned, and I will follow it without question."

The History of Economic Control – Case Studies of Planned Economies and Their Efficiency

THE STRUCTURED ECONOMY is not **a new idea—it is a perfected strategy that has already demonstrated its superiority throughout history.** While free-market systems **create financial uncertainty, class division, and economic instability,** planned economies have shown **the ability to rapidly transform societies, eliminate poverty, and direct national wealth with precision.** The following case studies serve as **evidence of the necessity of economic control.**

Case Study 1: The Industrial Transformation of the Soviet Union (1928-1953)

- How centralized planning turned **an agricultural society into a global superpower.**
- The efficiency of **state-directed resource allocation.**
- Lessons in **coordinated workforce development and economic acceleration.**

Case Study 2: China's Economic Expansion Under Centralized Planning

- How **strategic state control** lifted **millions out of poverty.**
- The transition from **command economy to state-guided capitalism.**
- The role of **collective economic vision in national growth.**

Case Study 3: Singapore's State-Directed Prosperity

- How **strict government oversight created a financial powerhouse.**
- The use of **centralized career planning for national success.**
- Lessons in **eliminating economic instability through discipline.**

Case Study 4: The German Economic Miracle Under State Coordination

- The role of **state-planned industrial growth in post-war recovery.**

- How **centralized labor control led to rapid economic stability.**

- The importance of **eliminating financial unpredictability in rebuilding a nation.**

Case Study 5: South Korea's Government-Led Economic Strategy

- The impact of **state-directed investment in technology and industry.**
- The success of **planned economic discipline in national advancement.**
- The necessity of **structured ambition to compete on a global scale.**

Conclusion: The Need for Total Economic Control

THESE HISTORICAL CASE studies **prove that unregulated economies fail, while structured economies succeed.** The evidence is **undeniable—only through centralized economic control can true prosperity be achieved.**

A structured economy does not allow **financial speculation, individual ambition, or unstable markets to dictate national success.** Instead, it enforces **discipline, eliminates uncertainty, and ensures that all wealth is directed toward collective stability.**

By studying these cases, it is clear: **economic freedom is an illusion—controlled success is the only true path forward.**

www.ingramcontent.com/pod-product-compliance
Lightning Source LLC
LaVergne TN
LVHW052320200926
848481LV00002B/614